CHAT BOUT

JAMAICAN DIALECT & ENGLISH POEMS BY JANICE HART

To my
Friend John
and photograph
Thanks a
Million

Yours and
Awesome
John's Cathy
4/4/18

AuthorHouse™
1663 Liberty Drive
Bloomington, IN 47403
www.authorhouse.com
Phone: 1 (800) 839-8640

Published by AuthorHouse 11/17/2017

ISBN: 978-1-5246-8937-7 (sc)
ISBN: 978-1-5246-8938-4 (e)
ISBN: 978-1-5462-1413-7 (hc)

Library of Congress Control Number: 2017906520

Print information available on the last page.

Any people depicted in stock imagery provided by Thinkstock are models,
and such images are being used for illustrative purposes only.
Certain stock imagery © Thinkstock.

This book is printed on acid-free paper.

Because of the dynamic nature of the Internet, any web addresses or links contained in this book may have changed
since publication and may no longer be valid. The views expressed in this work are solely those of the author and do not
necessarily reflect the views of the publisher, and the publisher hereby disclaims any responsibility for them.

Cover and Title Page Photographed by John Tangredi

Bank of Jamaica for the Bank Notes
The Jamaica Information Service for National Emblems and Symbols
National Heroes and History of Jamaica

authorHOUSE®

Author's Acknowledgement's

I wish to express my thanks through this medium to the following:

The late Honorable Dr. Louise Bennett OD, for being the forerunner of our Jamaican Culture and especially expressing her works through our people's language Patois (Patwa).

A special thanks to Mr. Harry Belafonte for your endearing words of strength and encouragement For being a trailblazer for Culture, Human Rights and your legacy in the world of entertainment.

Monty Alexander, for giving me the opportunity of sharing many stages with the Harlem to Kingston express Trio. For all the opportunities offered to me over the years that enhanced my art development and performances, Radio and Television shows, I truly appreciate.

Thanks to the legendary Calypso Rose and The Mighty Sparrow for giving me the opportunity to perform with them.

To John Tangredi for the Bank of Jamaica for the Bank Notes and The Jamaica Information Service for National Emblems and Symbols, National Heroes and History of Jamaica.

And the many unnamed supporters whose advice and criticism and appreciation have made my life work rewarding.

To my nine siblings, thanks for all your support through the years.

<u>HARRY G. BELAFONTE'S ACKNOWLEDGEMENT</u>

The richness of the culture of the island of Jamaica has touched the hearts and minds of many in the world. I am fortunate to be a descendant of that culture and nowhere has anyone reflected its beauty and power more aptly than Janice Hart does here. She is one of our great cultural historians. This book should bring you pleasure.

Harry Belafonte
January, 2017

2

A True Renaissance woman
Janice Hart "Miss Matty Lou"
Photographed by Simon Lewis

For most of us who grew up in Jamaica during the 1950's and 1960's, we had the opportunity to either learn about or see a performance of the island's cultural icon and poet, the late Louise Simone Bennett.

Known to her fans worldwide as Miss Lou, Bennett became the voice of the island's culture at home and abroad. A social commentator who liberally used Jamaican patois in her creations she brought an overwhelming talent to the stage, radio, television and movies.

Accepted by many as Jamaica's leading comedienne and the "only poet who has really hit the truth about her society through its own language," Bennett's passing in 2006 at the age of 86, was considered a great loss to the culture of the island that could never be replaced.

While they may be right with this conclusion, we who live in Connecticut and the New York areas, have been fortunate to have in our midst another Jamaican entertainer, Janice Marie Hart, whose performances many agreed could easily match that of Miss Lou. In fact, it is the belief of many that Hart who performs as "Miss Matty Lou," is just as talented as the legendary Miss Lou.

From Buff Bay, Portland, Jamaica, Janice who now lives in Hamden, Connecticut, like Miss Lou has kept the Jamaican culture alive and well. She is a phenomenal storyteller, poet, keynote speaker and diversity consultant-a true Renaissance Woman." You must not forget your roots" is one of her favorite sayings.

Janice, who thrills the audience wherever she performs, and has appeared on several television shows on CPTV, WFSB and WTNH has self- published her first book "CHAT BOUT," which is a concentration of poems written in Jamaican patois. Several articles have been published about her in the Jamaica overseas Gleaner and other local paper. Janice has been an invited guest to the White House during Caribbean Heritage month and performed one of her famous poems titled, "I am so glad you came."

A member of the Caribbean Cultural Theatre, she was the main artist in the Nine Night celebration for the late Miss Lou, Trevor Rhone and Rex Nettleford at St. Francis College in Brooklyn, New York. Janice is a member of The National Association of Professional Women.

Janice is the founder and lead singer of the Voices if the Caribbean, folklore group that is well respected in Hartford. Although her desire during her performances is to use the Jamaican dialect, Janice writes great poems and essays on world events, nature, inspiration, history, love and just about any topic you can imagine. She won an award from the Connecticut Hospital Association for an essay which she essay which she wrote titled "My First Trauma Experience."

If you are able to get to know her closer, you will find that she is a very versatile, compassionate, caring and helpful individual. Janice specializes in high performances team building and development, enlightened leadership development, interpersonal communications, dynamic cultural diversity development, organizational alignment and conflict resolution.

Janice, who holds a Master Degree in Theology, Bachelor Degree in Theology, an Associate Degree in Science, a Diploma in Business, Certificates in Advance Pastoral Counseling, Critical Decision Making, Mediation and Facilitation, is a mentor for young people. She is also an advisor and a true leader, a facilitator and mediator with the Community Dialogue of New Haven.

Janice is also an ordained Minister following the footsteps of her dad. A 27- year employee at Yale New Haven Hospital. She uses her talents to raise scholarship funds for minority students. She has been a beacon of strength in raising funds and goods for victims of hurricanes and earthquakes in the Caribbean.

For the past ten years she has single-handedly started to feed 100 people in shelters and half- houses during the Christmas Holidays and harsh winter months, with meals which she cooks herself. During that same time, she adopts 40 children from homeless shelters and with the help of friends gives each child self-wrapped gifts of clothing. Throughout the year she collects slightly worn clothing which she brings to different shelters. Janice volunteers her talent in mediation and facilitation to assist with halfway house residents transitioning back in society.

Over the years she has received numerous awards which includes the Dr. Martin Luther King Jr. award for exemplifying unity, community and respect for the uniqueness of others, Marcus Mosiah Garvey Award for Cultural Development, a Certificate from the State of Connecticut Office of the Treasury for Outstanding Service, one from the West Indian Foundation, Inc. for Outstanding Service and a Community Service Award from the West Indian Social Club of Hartford. Janice also won an award for the Best Oral Presentation from Workshop in Business Opportunity.

Contents

POEMS FROM THE SOUL

National Symbols

The Flag

Jamaica's flag was unveiled on Independence Day, August 6, 1962. The flag has a diagonal cross with four triangles in juxtaposition. The symbolism of the flag is: "Hardships there are, but the land is green and the sun shineth." As to the colors of the flag: black symbolizes the hardships overcome and to be faced, gold the natural wealth and beauty of sunlight, and green for hope and agricultural resources.

The Flower

"Lignum Vitae," a name supposedly adopted because of the plant's medicinal qualities, is indigenous to Jamaica.

The Bird

The "Doctor Bird" lives only in Jamaica and is one of the most outstanding of all species of humming-birds. The feathers of this bird are beautifully iridescent, a characteristic peculiar to the family.

The Fruit

The "Ackee" is an edible fruit (when ripe) which was brought to Jamaica from West Africa in the 18th century.

The Tree

The "Mahoe" is one of Jamaica's secondary economic timbers. Mahoe, popular with small furniture manufacturers as the attractive blue-green wood with variegated yellow intrusions, is capable of taking a high polish which shows up the variety of grain and color tones.

The Coat of Arms

The original Coat of Arms granted to Jamaica in 1661 was designed by the Archbishop of Canterbury, and apart from a partial revision in 1957, remains virtually the same. The Coat of Arms shows a male and female Arawak standing on either side of the shield, which bears a red cross with five golden pineapples superimposed on it. The crest is a Jamaican crocodile surmounting the Royal Helmet and Mantlings with the motto "Out of Many, One People."

OUT OF MANY, ONE PEOPLE

THE JAMAICAN EMBLEMS ARE – THE COAT OF ARMS, THE FLAG AND NATIONAL ANTHEM

THE JAMAICAN SYMBOLS ARE – THE BLUE MAHOE, HUMMING BIRD, LIGNUM VITAE & ACKEE

Famous Jamaican clichés

1. Nuh care how much powda yuh put pan black bud 'im still black.
You can't change someone's poor habits easily.

2. Yuh liddung wid dawg, yuh git up wid fleas.
Be careful of the people you associate with.

3. Wen yuh go a Jackass yaad, yuh noh fi chat bout im big ayse.
Don't criticize others in their presence.

4. Pretty roses got macca fi jook yuh.
There are two sides to every coin.

5. Yuh cyaan tek mout wata fi go out fiyah.
Always have what you need for the job

6. No sen a chigga foot man fi go mash macca.
You need the right tools to do the job.

7. Cow neva know de use a im tail till fly tek charge.
Know the value of what you have before you loose it.

8. Look before you leap.
Know where you are going before you go.

9. Farden pocket an' poun a cheese.
Know what you can afford before committing.

10. Yai bigger than stomach.
Biting off more than you can eat.

11. Wen jackass smell corn 'im gallop.
People respond to right encouragement.

12. Yuh cyaan stop flying crow fedda from drop, yuh can
hinder crow from mek nest pon yuh head top.
Control your own destiny.

13. Wen dawg flee bite yuh, yuh haffi scratch.
It's normal to respond to a stimulus.

14. Time neva too lang fi banabis grow beans.
Slow and steady does the job.

15. Cuss-cuss no bore hole eena mi skin.
Words cannot hurt me.

16. Before han' goh a mill, put trash
Avoid hurting yourself, when you are upset.

17. Look fi yuh black cow before night come
Know your pathway before it becomes dark.
18. Wen trouble tek yuh, pickney shut will fit yuh
Use what you have in time of crisis

19. Wat a fi yuh, cyan be un fi yuh
What is meant to be yours will be yours.

20. Cockroach nuh bizniz eena fowl yaad
Do not meddle in thinhgs that does not concern you.

21. Young bud don't know storm
Experience teaches wisdom

22. Dawg a sweat him long hair cover it.
You can't judge someone's troubles by their appearance.

23. Rock stone deh a riva bottam, cyan know sun hot
He who feels it knows it.

24. Every dawg have dem day, an' every puss got dem four O' clock

25. Man nuh dead nuh call him duppy
Never count out someone when they are down on their luck.

26. One, one coco full basket
Every little bit adds up to much.

27. Man bawn fi heng cyan drown.
You cannot escape your destiny

28. Duppy know who fi frighten
People have the tendency to take advantage of those who seems easy going.

29. Chicken merry, hawk deh near
Danger is often closeby when you are having too much fun.

30. De higha de monkey climb, de more he expose
You become more vulnerable when your status increases, as in a promotion

32. Play wid puppy, puppy dem will lick yuh nose
Familiarity breeds contempt

33. Wah sweet nanny goat a goh run him belly
You can have too much of a good thing

34. Every hoe ha dem tick a bush
There is a perfect mate for everyone, even the most unlikely person

35. Ole fiya tick easy fi ketch
It's easy to rekindle an old romance

36. Puss an' dawg nuh have de same luck
Some people are luckier than others.

37. Wen dawg have money him buy cheese.
When there is excess money sometimes we spend it foolishly

38. A rabbit cyan weigh more dan him quarter
Everything in life has specific value.

39. Circumstances alter cases, mek jackass wear braces
Adapting to immediate changes.

40. Wen ashes get cold, dawg liddung in it.
Taking advantage of a situation.

41. Every coconut have dem own shell.
There is a place for everything in life.

42. Don't mess wid mawga cow, coulda bull mumma.
Do not underestimate simply looking people, you have no idea who they are connected to.

43. Nuh expect pig fi bawk, 'im only grunt
Don't be surprised when a pig grunts that's the sound he
makes. Don't be surprised by others behavior.

44. Sake a fish open mout' 'im get ketch everytime
Talking too much will get you in trouble everytime.

45. Ben' tree wen it young, yuh cyan ben' ole tree, it will bruk.
Train your children when they are young and pliable, it will be too late when they are grown.

46. A nuh lack a tongue mek cow nuh talk.
Don't repeat everything you hear.

47. Noh mek yuh lef' han' know wat yuh right han' a do.
It's best to keep a secret from those who are close to
you.

48. Lawn fi dance a yaad before yuh dance abraad.
Practice your craft at home, before performing in public.

49. Yuh life lang but yuh cayliss wid it.
Know when situations are too risky for you.

50. Ah nuh de same day leaf drap inna wata it ratten.
Sometimes mistakes made in the past catches up with you later in life.

A FI WI LUV BIRD

A nuh chi,chi, yellow, galling, john crow, groundove
Or any species a bud yuh know
A fi wi luv bird.

Mi nuh waan fi hear anybaddy
A bad mout wi airline
'cause a it a de whole a wi lifeline
ah nuff odder fancy airline service
mi si tap brap an lef dem passenger hi an dri
some even lef dem hi eena sky
but nuh wi luv bird.

Yuh can bet pan yu nice hot meal
Sunday dinna a still rice an peas
Durin de week yu get all de likes
Curry ram goat, brown stew chicken
An don't figet de national dish
Our ackee an salt fish.den to tap it off
Champagne an wat 'ave yu.

Some a oonu pass oonu place an call it market bus
I really don't care it a de bes in de air.
De girl dem still pretty an brite same way
An de bwoy dem well ansome dem self.
As fi de touris dem luv de feelings of home

So dem tek de luv bird for de people
Just a chat an galang like dem eena dem living room.

Nohf pass yuh place wid Jamaican people
For wen it come to xtra baggage, wi a de gagan fi it.
Wi carry home wi six month old niece, nephew,
Granpickney or smaddy pickney, just fi de xtra baggage.
No mek de attendant ax wi a who de xtra baggage belong to
Wi tell dem sey a fi de baby tings,
Wen a ongle one pampa wi stuff eena wi hanbag fi de baby.
Soh 'Butch Stewart' wi really want fi tenk yuh
Fi making wi 'ave wi owna airline.

So nex time yu deh plan fi come home
Tek de ongle Luv Bird wid de brightest color in de sky
Air Jamaica wid de hummin' bird pan de tail side.
An memba sey a smaddy hafi lift up dem deh
Bag an pan yuh deh put pan plane
Yuh cyaan carry home 'Merica all de time.

As mi granny woulda sey
What is fi yuh cyan be un-fi-yuh.

DE JAMAICAN AIRBUS

A FI YUH BIZNIZ

I want fi know who a go buy
Because everyone got sinting fi sell
From I was bawn till now
Or from Independence of 1962
I neva witness so much people a sell.

Higlering tun big bizniz
Everybaddy got forein tings a sell
From a pin to ah anka.

Yuh know Jamaica boast a wedda
Of 85degree all year roun'
Imagine yuh can get long boots
Fur coats an' gloves wid scarves to match
For my people ongle buy tings in set.

My Jamaican people will sell
Any an everyting because
Smaddy de fi buy it.

I pass mi place go ax a peddler
Why all dese winta tings
Shi look pan mi awful strange
An ax mi if mi neva hear bout
The Jamaican Bobsled team.

An' dat was all I need to know,
Gloves, scarves, mittens, long boots
Crismus a come once a year
Come get yuh winta wear.

As mi granny woulda sey
If yuh walk barefoot,
Yuh mustn faas wid macca.

BIG AND BEAUTIFUL

Lawks gi mi pass fi si de beauty queen dem a parade
Look pan de size a she, a weh she a try win,
Miss Berta have one dawta name beauty
An' she is very much eena dis competition.

But as yuh an mi know, beauty is in de yeye of de beholder
For I don't know ef dem noh si
How de gal ayse cock off like poodle
An' har yeye fava pattoo.

Missis yuh si dem deh foot
A mus Kingston she a represent
For dem is capital K and har knee cup a mek nise
She definitely a starve herself.

Well here dem come fi de swim suit part
Yuh can si anyting dem almost naked
Dis part should name de skin suit competition
For a so so skin dem a show.

Gatha all lakka mi an yuh wid wi robustus self
Dem wouldn't have noh where fi wi model
Wat a sinting dat would be
Wi should start something fi wi self
An' call it plus size jamboree.

As mi granny woulda sey beauty is only skin deep
But ugly is to de bone.

So all ah oonu big people kip heart
For dere is coming a day wen plus size model
Will rule de worl' stage.

BIG NIGHT

What a gran splendacious night
The Caribbean people put on dem
Pretty, pretty mek up dem face
Put on dem expensive perfume.
Here dem come eena dem pinted toe,
Square toe, spike eel boot, wedge eel
And sling back shoes.
Dis is a night of celebration dem well deserve.
As big bwoy sey wah eena teecha book
It eena fi mi to.
Massah tap yah lickle,
Cuh pan dat de foot eena de spike eel shoes
Noh size twelve she need, dat fava ten an a half.
A how she manage fi squeeze fi har foot eena it
Ef she tink she bad mek she tek off de shoes.
Mi bet yuh all mi gat it neva fit har back
But anyway a faas mi faas, for fi mi hair piece
A gi mi hell, I feel like hag eena harness
Mi noh 'ave much time tonight
For de night noh belang to mi
So all ah oonu lovely people out dere
Tenk yuh an oonu all look bononous.
As mi granny woulda sey
Don't go eena quart can, wen pint can ole yuh.

CELEBRATING GOVERNOR GENERAL, HOWARD COOKE 80th BIRTHDAY

CIRCULA' FONE A YAAD

Bwoy dem people who invent cellphone
Mus did know sey Jamaicans would be dere
Number one customa.
I bus' outa laffin' de odder day, wen I hear a cellphone
A ring pan a donkey hampa,
An' I si shorty wid four cellphone, pan 'im waist.

Now shorty is a small bizniz man
Who operate 'im owna han' truck service to market higgla
Ef yuh don't know wat dat is, mek mi explain it to yuh.
'im cyaah dem goods from eena market
an' load dem pan Vinny big Bedford truck fi country.

But as yuh know Shorty got 'im own rules,
Yuh don't 'ave to pay unless yuh call 'im
An' a soh comes 'im got all a de customa dem.
Yuh neva si smoke widdout fiya.

For as yuh know most higgla a big time trixter.
Afta Shorty load dem pan de big truck dem climb up
An' ah ell 'im next week.
Miss Gatha tink she a de smartest, an dis week mek two
She look like she figet ah who name shorty.

For eena fi mi book dem coulda easy call 'im long tongue.

Shorty decide dis ya week nah pass an' 'im noh get pay.
So gatha 'im yell out, yuh nah go 'ome tidday ef yuh noh pay mi.
So shorty lay dung in front a fi vinny truck an' a cuss fi 'im money.

Wat a scene, for yuh know sey trouble jus' start
For vinny wid fi 'im ignorant stamma self get wind ah de story.
One piece ah stammering started, missis yuh had to be present
Quick a clock miss gatha find shorty money before fiasco bruk out.

As mi granny woulda sey
Stop quarrel before fight come.

CIRCULA' FONE SALESMAN, HALF WAY TREE, JAMAICA

CRISMUS YAAD STYLE

Dis ya experience ya funny fi true, ef yuh neva go home fi Crismus
Yuh might not undastan.
A wi' try mi very best fi mek mi pint real clear an' de picture perfect.
Miss Clara afta livin' eena 'Merica so long, mi decide fi go home, fi mi fus Crismus.
Wen mi ketch ah airport a mek sure I was very early
Soh mi check in pan time, but widin five minutes ah swear sey ah was eena flea market.
People was dc go home an' ef yuh si bag 'n' pan, Aqueduct or Thuderbird
flea market noh got so much venda pan de busiest weekend.
People a travel from age zero to one hundred
Because yuh an' mi know is a good time fi carry down smaddy pickney fi get de xtra baggage.
Mi notice sey di people dem at Air Jamaica had all dem check in counta open.
Some a dem a smile wid yuh an' lickle small talk
While some a dem look bex like de cold wedda de badda dem.
Wen mi get pan de plane mi had to laff wen one a de stewardess sey de flight was full,
Ah wanda ef shi noh realize sey a Decemba 19th an' everybaddy an' dem granny de go home.
De captain neva need fi turn on de TV for we had our own in flight entertainment.
Pickney de halla an' bawl f idem real mumma, granny de worry 'bout har han' luggage.
One young man him de cuss because dem tek wey him carry on bag wid him
fraggle items because it was too big. One woman de faas an'sey because him neva
want fi pay fi xtra baggage, him kindly tell har fi fix har blonde weave.
Odda people pan dem cell phone a tell dem fambly how far dem reach eena
flight wen de plane still pan de tarmac. Fi wi people a one of a kind.
Miss Clara a don't know who invent cell-phone, but dem shoulda
call it "hell phone" for a so so chaos it cause.
Dem want wi fi buckle up now, soh mi wi see yuh wen mi lan.
Look fi mi eena de bright red pants suit wid mi long white boots, gloves
and mi London fog for mi hear sey cold front a pass dung deh.
Merry Crismus yaad style.

Aye ya yai.

CUSS OUT

A wah yuh sey gal
Is mi who yuh waan fi trace
Mi is jus de one,fi set yuh strait
An' put yuh eena yuh place.

Kuh how yuh fava heng pon nail
Si yah gal mi an yuh nuh combolo
Yuh si mi a walk solo
De las time mi si sinting lakka yuh
Was mascarade night.

Yuh fava jonkunnu
A don't know weh a ole ramgutang
An ole jezebel, go weh
Yuh gat farden hair an' poun a hair piece.
A wanda a how much horse tail
Dem tek fi mek fi yuh piece.

Ef yuh nuh like wah mi sey
Kirrout gal an gwaan yuh ways
Yuh smell like wen abscess
Bruk unda johncrow wing.
Yuh han full a ring
An yuh cyaan do a ting.

A mussa nite time,wen yuh fine smaddy
An pray hard sey, day noh light too soon,
For wen 'im tek one look pan yuh
Ef 'im heart string no good 'im mus fall dung.
'im gwine swear 'im si duppy
so galang yuh ways an tenk, de man who create mekup
For noh mek daylight yuh widdout it.

As mi granny woulda sey
Tongue double brings trouble.

DE COUNTRY BUS

A weh de bus deh so lang
Tap de mah, a wah coulda wrong
Look ya I jus a bruck de corna
De duco pan I chippy, chippy like ole innamel basin.

Dem mus be noh know people deh pan has'e
An noh gat noh time fi was'e
Kuh 'ow de bus deh crawl
Like coot a cum outa crawl pan.

Mi nearly drop offa de step
Eena dis ya obble skirt mi deh wear
Lawks Rose mi hear a split
A tear it deh tear
Step up eena de bus ya ma
Ah who tell yuh fi wear dat.

Some a wi noh know wi age or size
Wi a dress like wi a go pan stage for big performance.
A beg yuh pardon sah, a wah yuh sey.
Yuh toe dem fava chicken hawk foot
Eena pinted toe boot.
Ef yuh know wah mi know no badda tek mi on.

Move up eena de bus

Nuff more people woulda like
Fi reach a dem work to.
Missis dem yah people deh push up
Dem mout like when mongoose
A sniff fi fowl nest.

Weh dem noh buy cyar ef dem
No waan fi travel pan bus.
Look ya man no draw mi tung
Eena de early mawning.
Drive up ya mi driver
Kingston far but it pretty.
As mi granny woulda sey
Lickle bit a ram goat 'ave beard
An big bull no ave non.

DE JAMAICAN BOBSLED TEAM

Yuh neva hear sey wi lickle but we tallawah
Nuh put nuting pass wi Jamaican
For wi is jus de one fi tell you
De last four letter in de word
Jamaican says ICAN.

Wi tek dem Olympics people by surprise
Dem coulda neva eena dem wildest dream
Tink wi coulda come up
Wid a bobsled team.

Dem mek de mistake an put it
Eena wi head an two, twos
Wi went right into gear
Wi start fi figure out
Wat a bobsled look like
An wah it good fa.

Boops wi fine out.
Den how wi fi qualify widout snow
But fi wi people are de fathers of ingenuity
Yes, wi get a ting togedda
Go up some dirt hill
An' dis was de end of de beginning.

Massa de rest is history
Wi ketcha Olympics an ef wi did 'ave
Money fi buy one state a de art bobsled
Dem know,wi woulda runway
Wid de fus prize or any odder prize dem gat,
For a soh wi tan.

As usual wi bruk record eena everyting
An dem did 'ave fi mek movie an books
Fi all ah oonu who neva believe,
Well we ketch a winta Olympics.

As mi granny woulda sey
Ef yuh want good yuh nose affi run.

DE JAMAICAN HIGLER

Guinep, guinep some a dem sour
Some a dem sweet
But dem come offa de same tree
De one to de East is de sweetest one
De one to de West is de sourest one.

Oranges, pineapples, bananas
Mi 'ave all de fruits yuh need.
Fi keep healty an' sweet an strong
No blame ef dem lickle brakish
An nuh mi mek den
A buy mi buy dem an dem grow pan tree

Hi nice man buy something from mi nuh sah
Nuh come feel up mi sinting dem
Ef yuh nah buy,weh yuh tap fa.
Nobaddy nah go want fi buy dem
Wen dem get saafy,saafy.

Massa mi nuh 'ave change fi dat
Mi nuh bruk mi ducks from mawning
Go weh yuh faas an' facey to,
Ah it mek mi nuh love come a Town market.

For oonu town people tink sey

Higler get dem goods fi free
Or lickle an nuting
Oonu don't even know dew wata.

Sweet guinep, oranges, pineapple
Bananas, mango,an' jackfruit
Dem is all so sweet
Come get yuh nice fruits fi eat.

As mi granny woulda sey
De more yuh chop breadfruit root,
De more im spring.

CURRY MAN, HIGHGATE MARKET, ST. MARY, JAMAICA

DE HAUNTED MARKIT PLACE

Miss Connie yuh hear smaddy de clear dem troat
Tap yuh dreaming yah missis
Yuh nuh si sey a late nite ma
Dem odder one always sey butcha Jones
Shh rollin calf haunt Porty market all nite.

Yuh si mi dying trials
De tings people 'ave fi go thru
Fi ketch early sales a market
I don't know who mek up de frase
'bout early bud ketch de mos' werm
But dem no tell yuh all de trouble
weh early bud ketch.

Mi feel like mi head de raise
A ongle when yuh si duppy, yuh head fi raise
Shhh tek time look out a yuh corna yai
Nuh ole Jones duppy dat a de meat stall
Wha 'im deh do ova deh si dung
Mi ting too heavy yah now fi talk.

Mi de go try fi shet mi yai
I cyan wait fi daylite
De next time mi come a Porty Markit
Mi nah go play cheap an' sleep unda market stall
Mi deh go rent one cheap room near de ded house.
Si yuh wen daylite yah Miss Connie.

As mi granny would a sey
Crab nuh trus nuh shado afta dark.

DEM LUV BRAATA

Yuh si mi dying trial Miss Matty
Mi tiyad a cuzin Sue an' har beggy, beggy
Every Satiday dem come a market
And wait till late come.

Dem visit every stall an' pretn' like dem a buy
Dem pick out few piece a food an' have de nerve
Fi a beg fi braata, like regula custama
Dem tink country higla ah idiat.

Mi ketch on pon dem game Matty an' now de game ova
By de time dem lef' market dem bankra loaded wid food
Dem noh pay fa.

Soh mek mi tell de whole a oonuu as of now noh come next week Wen market
ova, cause wi a lef' massa Braata home neva fi him come back a town
Soh come a market before sundown.

As mi granny woulda sey, everyday yuh carry bucket goh a well,
one day de battam ago drop out an' everyting crash?

37

DE PORTLAN' BANANA MAN

De rain come wet wi
De sun come bun wi
But I nah tap wi
"Cause wi a de Portlan banana man.

Thru de Portlan' rain and mud, mud
We deh go reap wi banana
Pan de donkey back wi gaan
Kutty kap, kutty kap up the hillside an' dung de gully.

For wi mus' bring the load come a low lan,
Weh wi can pak dem on pon Mass George ole Bedford truck.
Tek yuh time wid mi gross Mitchell
A nuff effort an time I tek mi an dem
Fi reach right ya so.

Nuh badda wid yuh ramgutang self
An' bruise mi banana head
Shorty lay dem easy pan de katta me mek.
Mek sure yuh nuh mix dem up wid Mass Joe
'Im 'ave lakatan an mi 'ave grossmitchell.

Easy dung de rocky road missa driva
Yuh got delicate cargo on board
De ship a wait eena de 'arbor
Wid de tallyman ready fi tally mi banana.

De rain a fall like flood a come
But wi use to it,'cause wi a de Portlan banana man.

As mi granny woulda a sey
Han go, packy come.

DE WEDDIN DAY

Kuyah puppa I neva si anytin
Like dis from I was bawn
Miss Mary baff han' gal, fine man fi marry shi.
De gal cyan even bwile saaf egg.

De weddin party dress to pus back foot
Dem ya tangerine color bridesmaid frock
De blind man coulda si dem a nite
Everybaddy a fan eena de lickle church.

De church neva 'ave so much people eva
De parson tek out 'im book
An begin fi marry de couple
But a who tell 'im fi go ax question
Him ax ef anybaddy object to de marriage.

A yah I deh, one gal shi halla out
Mi is 'im baby madda an' sweetheart.
Miss Mary baff han gal cyan cook a ting
Hungry gwine kill de po man
So gi 'im some time fi mek up 'im mine.

De parson start fi bus cold sweat
For nuhbaddy neva stop 'im wediin yet
But de groom yell out mi cyan cook
So mi wi teach mi baffhan wife.

Den de boat a dem swap de ring
An eena one corus dem sey darling Ido.

As mi granny woulda sey
Woman luck de a dungle heap
Fowl go cratch I out.

DEAR MI SUGGA PLUM

Mi gizzada, mi sweet biskit, mi neva know a coulda mis yuh like dis.
Wen ah wake up dis mawning an' a realize sey yuh gaan.
Mi heart heart start pan one galloping like ass pan Caymans track
A dat deh time mi deh realize how much yuh mean to mi.
Like how hag love mud, mud an' every jub, jub cheese got 'im moley bread
Ah soh mi an' yuh will stay togedda until one a wi part.
Soh yuh memba de day yuh tell mi how much yuh love mi
Like how puss love butta an ants love aft. Ah ongle hope yuh did
Really mean wah yuh sey. For mi sin oh big writa fi start
But mi wi try fi explain myself. Look to di right han' corna
An' use dat piece a string fi measure yuh luv fi mi
Roun' yuh ring finga pan yuh lef't han'.
Den ax smaddy fi hold one end of it an dat ah de size
A de house yuh wi have fi mek dere is lot more tings fi explain
An' wat mi cyaan spell mi wi draw. So wah yuh nuh figga ut miwi show yuh.
Rememba sey mi love yuh wid all a mi heart an' soul.
Xoxoxoxoxoxox.

As mi granny woulda sey
Everybaddy got dem smaddy.

DEF AYSE GAL

Miss Dinah a weh de def ayse gal yuh gat deh,
From mawning de gal git up an gaan a ribba
Sey she de go wash clothes
Mi no bless mi yai pan ar since dat.
A mus a everybaddy eena de districk clothes shi de
wash, A soon tree.a. clack an shi no come back yet.
Yuh si de rain a set up a country mah
Wen dat bus open yuh know it naa tap.
From I was bawn I neva si smaddy ayse haad soh !
Dis yah gal cyaan live lang
For shi naa listen to nobaddy,
So .im mus feel.
Yessiday mi sen de gal go buy, de meat fi dinna
Shi come back next to nite.
So me sey mi naa mek noh nite dinna
So nobaddy no nyam.
Mi deh plan fe har oh
Jus like how ole ooman
A sware afta gumma bean
Gumma bean a sware fi run ole ooman belly.
As mi granny woulda sey
Hard aiyse pickney pay twice

DISCOVA YAAD

Miss Dinah dis as always been
A puzzle fi mi an. many village lawyers
I don.t know how hist.ry .ave it recorded,
Dat fi wi islan was discova in 1494
By one lickle man an .im combolo
All de way from .Italy.name Christifa Columbus.
As mi nuh edicated or historian
Mi want some ah oonu fi 'elp mi investigate
Dis ya ole hist'ry,de people dem call demself
Voyager, discoverer, an' sailor
Come tek charge a fi wi country Jamaica
Well Massa a deh worl war start
For wi resent dem occupation an' new culture,
Dem kill out de poor lickle
Aborigines of de islan.
De Arawak an' Caribe Indians.
An. a it mek dem affi go import
De Africans an. start de slave trade bizniz
Dat ended eena heepa war
For wi start de fight fi freedom
So next time wen yuh hear smaddy
A talk bout fi wi Jamaican hist'ry
Tell dem pan de top a yuh lungs sey
Nobaddy nuh discova,wi eena 1494
For wi was neva lass, wi was quite contented

Wid wi simple way of life
Wi did always know wi self
A buck dem cum buck wi up.
As mi granny would a sey
Wen yuh go a jackass yaad,
yuh nuh fi chat .bou 'im big aise.

MISS MATTY LOU AND SISTERS JENNIFER & HALCY

FOREIGN PRICES

Mi noh know a weh dem people yah get dem ideology
from Missis tek time wid dem deh big wuds deh yah Ma
Ah it mek dem want fi charge oonu foreign people tourist price.
A it mi come yah fi ax yuh bout
A who fa idea was dis
Because mi noh know a which Jamaican
Who live a foreign ago come ya fi visit
An' pay tourist price eena dem own a country.
Noh matter how dem speaky,spokey an twang wen
dem lan Ef yuh eva go mek mention bout different price
fi pay Yuh cyaant chat patois wussara dan dem.
Miss Gatha mi si a couple pull up a
Dunns Riva toder day an' mi know sey dem a foreigner
Yuh know how people smell wen dem come from
'Merica. But wen dem ketch wind a de price list
De woman tell de man she will buy de tickets
Because de man talk patois wid a lickle foreign flava.

So she go up to de winda an tell de cashier
Sell mi two adult ticket.
A believe de cashier smell har parfum
An' go ax har if she live ya
Mi noh know ef yuh eva buck up eena wasp nest
Eena sun hot, well mi noh haffi tell yuh
De woman hawl out har tongue an' de rest is history.
Don.t question my Jamaican people wen dem come fi
visit An spen dem haad earn winta dollars fi .ave fun.
As mi granny woulda sey
Mek sleeping dawgs lie dung
For yuh noh know ef him .ave rubba teet.

GRAN' MARKET

Crismus come again an mi noh get notting
De pickney dem want pretty, pretty
Toys an' games an' sinting.
Po mi gal noh know weh fi start or begin.

De two nanny mi hide unda de dressa draw
Cyan buy all me waan
Wat a pressure Crismus bring
Gi presents cook nuff food an 'ave plenty fi drink.

Dat ongle easy fi people who 'ave it
Poor people like mi no 'ave notting
Crismus is no fun, wen belly a growl,
An' pickney need everyting.

Right now it nuh matta, wah smaddy gi mi
Will be appreciated
It nuh easy wen yuh nuh 'ave notting
An' crismus come.

Si one cyar pull up outa gate mamma
De smaddy fava Auntie Katie
But nuh some twenty years pass
Wi nuh hear a wud from har.

Mi mus a si doubles, smaddy pinch mi
A how shi coulda find mi eena disya
Backa wall tenament yaad
A dis yuh call crismus mirricle.

A shi fi true, kiss mi neck
Auntie Katie yuh mek wi crismus
Mi nah gi up 'ope no more
De Lord will always provide.

As mi granny would a sey
Wah nuh dead, nuh call it duppy.

HURRICANE GILBERT

A bex till mi heart string nearly bus
De two people dem pounce pan mi
An' I start fi cuss, I cyan stan' wen people
Tek mi fi idiat.
Dem neva ax mi noh question
Dem ongle mek assumption
An missis mi .ave fi tell yuh de res
People I will neva understan.
Gilbert blow an tek off mi roof
Mi nice courts dresser, wardrobe, and chest of draws
Went flyingt down de road
Dinah mi whole life belongings
Disappear before mi very yeye.
But mouti, mouti tell mi sey
Help a come from overseas
So mi fine myself a de meeting place
To see wat mi could get.
An wen mi hear people start
Wid dem list of missing tings
A realize dis was pon a larger scale

Dan mi poor gal tink
I barrow mass luter pencil an start mi list
One BMW, two MINIVAN, mi precious market
Hancart mek from scratch, mi Gucci jewelry
Mi name bran clothes an' mi HITCHCOCK furniture.
Eh how could I figet mi satellite dish an computer
Mi DELL laptop
By de time I done wid dem an mass Gilbert
I get back everyting an' some.
So no mek nobaddy fool yuh
A noh lickle bad name de poor bwoy
Gilbert get fi notting
Dung to some pickney dat bawn.
As mi granny woulda sey
Trouble deh a bush, anancy cyaah it unda yuh bed.

INDEPENDENCE DAY AUGUST 6, 1962

Wat a bam-bam Miss Vashti yuh hear wah deh gwaan
Jamaica gat independence from Englan' tiday August 6, 1962
Wat a celebration, everbaddy a jump up eena great jubilation
Wi attack Englan' like a bull by de horn an' tell her fi set wi free
From de bans of fi dem history and dem hierchay
Dem memba how Queen Nanny ambush an' beat de life out an Englishman
, soh dem tell wi fi gwaan, cause a long time wi deh chase people out a wi islan'
Although nuff a wi was Englan' bound an still love de queen an her Poun' freedom come fus
All dem heepa free sinting wi use to get from Englan' gwine stop tonight
Miss Vasshti, dem exercise book wid de King an' Queen pan di cover,
Free Issue Not to Be Sold dat done a hope oonu know
Wi realize wi did have fi wi own heroes an smaddy fi lead wi own country, Englan'
did lickle bit too far fi si wah really deh gallang, soh yes wi mek wi own decision,
soh all a oonu Johnny come lately noh tek independence soh lightly
Lawd de union jack a lower right now and the Independent flag Yellow fi di natural wealth and
beauty of sunlight, de green fi the hope and agricultural resources, Black fi all de strength and
creativity of the people ;a rise up right now blowing in the high Jamaican wind, wat a beauty
Eternal father Bless Our Land Guide us with thy mighty hand, wat a feelings, all de lickle
pickney dem a get some aluminum cup wid fi wi own coat of arms while grown-ups a get
crockery plate and teapot yuh memba de excitement an' celebration, music a blast from duke box
and sound system wat a ataclaps pan mi poor gal tinite, johnkoonu or mascaraed, dancehall a
mash up de place, Church Service to give God Thanks, people a get married an' baby a bawn
Mek yuh Mumma teach yuh true Respect fi all an' it might stir yuh respond to duty call, For
Jamaica land we love from de rolling hills of lush green Portland to de Flatlands of Westmoreland.
As mi granny woulda sey;
Don't mess wid de mumma alligator till yuh cross river.

ITAL JUICE MAN

Strong back, double trouble, Irish moss
Front end lifter, peanut punch, Zion
Eight furlong, tan pan I long
All natural juices
Come one an' all, come get yuh juice.
Mi .ave all de natural tonic drinks
Yuh bady need
Look yah Massa yuh coulda
Do well wid almost everyting mi sell,
Nuh tek nuh liberty wid me yah sah
Time too haad.
A how fi yuh bady run run dung
An' so mash up
Yuh fava lakka wen John Crow
De bake plantain fi yuh
A how yuh allow yuhself fi get so
Massa yuh nuh gat mirror a yuh yaad.
Juice man ova here
Come get yuh double trouble yah so
It wi mek yuh good eena yaad wuk
An' yuh won.t affi worry bout Mass Joe.
Yuh know Joe grine, im same one.
A who yuh a tek on juice man
Mi did ax yuh fi any help
Anyway a wah yuh seh it will do fi mi,

Sell mi two strong back an' double trouble.
Strong back, root drinks, natural juices
Dem is all de I an I mek
Tenk yuh sah.
As mi granny woulda sey,
No everyting weh got sugar a sweet.

HIGHGATE MARKET, ST. MARY, JAMAICA

KEROSENE DE KING PAN

A plenty a oonu figet de versatility of de kerosene five gallon pan of coconut oil
Jamaican used de pan mostly a country fi carry and store kerosene oil fi lamp, stove, bokkle torch
and all other use. A soh come it was called kerosene pan. Once Jamaican put a name pan something
or somebaddy it stick fi life. Shopkeepers neva have han' fi sell de empty pan to. There were time
wen it cause vexation.

But de most valuable use of thc kerosene or zinc pan was wen it was discova to be a cook pot for wood
fiya or coal stove. As fi wi, it was de pan fi bwile hog food, but believe mi goat head soup, corn pork
banana, yellow yam and flour dumplin' taste the best when cooked in dis Zinc pan.

My auntie Rose from Alva St Ann could steam white rice or rice an' peas into de Zinc pan an' it noh
bun, dat a skill. Come wedding, nine night, dance or any kind a celebration a row of zinc pan could
be seen lined up on old flat spring from dem Morris oxford or Austin Cambridge car on rock stone
across 3ood fire looking like a Viking stove.

A nuff a wi from Portland carry wata eena zinc pan widdut kata pan wi head, a it mek de top part a
wi head ball to dis day. De Zinc pan was used on wshing day fi bwile white clothese so dem would
come out lilly white, a bet nuff a yuh readin' dis neva had dis experience. Lawd country life was de
best. Yuh had to understand how to treat de zinc pan soh it noh rust up yuh clothes.

Soh enamel pan, aluminum pan, plastic tubs Mr. Kerosene (Zinc Pan) was de fore runner fi all ah
oonu. Soh give respect to zinc pan an' put him dung eena Jamaica History Book as King of all Pans.
As mi Granny woulda sey, new broom sweep clean, but old broom know de corner.

MI DEH COME HOME

Dear Mi Sista, how is tings going
Ah hope everybody is keepin' well.
Ef smaddy did tell mi a soh life
Haad a foreign
I woulda stan a country weh I did deh.
For nottin' wasn't wrong wid de ole
Kitchen out a door,de rusty zinc sower
A de stan pipe, an' de pit tilet.
For as yuh know it was fi mi job fi kip it spic an span
An' presentable at all times especially pan Sunday's wen
Parson use to stop by.
Mi deh wanda ef ah it mek mi did come weh
Pan Housekeepin' work.
It noh easy fi be some people maid.
For dem is too bold face an' farad.
Dem tell mi sey mi fi ongle clean de house
An' wash clothes an so on.
But sista fi seven years now mi noh get a raise
An' mi deh notice sey de Missis deh breed.
An' mi noh plan fi nurs' noh pickeney
Pan de same money, soh mi deh come home.
Yuh memba wen Busta an' Garvey did create
Union back eena de day's fi protect wi a yaad.
It seems like wi need one fi housekeepas right ya so.
Wah yuh tink mi fi do?
Lawks soh much taut a cross mi mine.
Tell mi sometin' mi cow Mae have any calf yet?

Dat deh cow mussa barren like fi Dinah lickle dung grow pig.
But cow or calf mi deh pack up mi tings.
All I will need is a small room fi put dung mi single bed
An' de wash stan'. Ah hope yuh neva dash wey or sell
Mi bed mi lef unda yuh cella'.Mi still have de two dulcimenia grip.
I know fi sure not anedda winta gwine ketch mi yah.
Noh mek nohbaddy fool yuh, money naah grow pan tree yah.
Ah it mek de letta yah soh dry,
Wen I return I will be able fe demands a good job fi suit
Mi edication as a professional home maker train
A foreign wid mi twang.
Ah know sey a lickle long winded,
Soh a mus' sey good-bye fi now.
Tek care a yuhself an Mass Joe an sell butcha Maben
Mae mi cow an' save mi piece a cornbeef.
As mi granny woulda sey, noh buy puss eena bag.

MY MOTHER'S BIRTH HOME, ALVA ST. ANN, JAMAICA

'MERICA NOH ALL DAT'

Dear Mi Sista,

De las time mi talk to yuh, yuh deh halla how 'Merica cold an' yuh cyaan
stan' winta noh more.Sista mi noh know wey mek yuh noh come home
even fi de Crismus an feel some ole time sun pan yuh skin.
Nuttin' much noh change a yaad since yuh go weh far yuh neva did kip yuh promise so
wi still have de out side tilet an' kitchen an mi know sey yuh get 'custom to warm wata
fi bade an' cold drinks eena frige but mi cyaan't afford JPS so noh lite nuh de yah.
But all dem inconvenience should'nt badda yuh.
Because afta thirty years a forein yuh mus cyaan book yuhself eena 'otel wid ease.
But sometin' a tell mi sey yuh soun'like yuh brok'. Soh ef yuh nuh 'ave nuh money try
yuh bes' stan right wey yuh deh. Yuh memba de lickle runted hag name Sue, she nyam
off all de piglet she did 'ave soh wi had no choice but fi nyam har. Anyway ef yuh still
decide fi come home fi de Crismus yuh fi mek mi know early for dere is a few tings
mi woulda like yuh to bring fi mi and de seven pickney, mi gat widdout puppa.
Yuh can call mi pan mi circular 'cause mi nuh 'ave noh credit pan it.
I close wid lots of love an' hope fi si yuh soon.

Yuh loving Sista,
Mae-Mae

MOUTI MOUTI

A lang time mi noh meet smaddy
Who dip dem mout eena everybaddy bizniz
An' fi dem bizniz de pwile.

Miss Tiny she go from yaad to yaad
A cyaah news, sey, sey story.
De las time shi get eena mix up story
Shi tell Miss Vie sey, dat Lena sey
Mass Joe tief Sammy goat.

So wen shi ketch a pass
De ole a dem gang up pan har
An' start fi trace har off.
An' yuh know de size a Vie mout'.

Shi get pan de defense of har man
An begin fi tell dem a weh
Wata walk go a pimpkin gut.

Miss Lena sey a noh dat she tell Tiny
She haad a hearing an' ben a try
Fi read har lip an' due to how shi
Did tek out har false teet
De wuds dem neva come out right.

Yuh can imagine de huffing an' puffing
An who naah beat up dem chess
A defen dem self eena people sey, sey

But a faas Miss Tiny faas
Yuh cyaan do nuting eena
Hopeful village mek shi ketch wind ah it
An it mek dem call har gleana.

Mi gaan a mi yaad
Before mi get eena people sey,sey.
Night a come.
As mi granny would a sey
A cock mout kill cock.

OBEAH MAN

Everbaddy know a obeah man
Ef yuh head hat yuh
An' yuh 'ave a bad dream
Or dat miss Jane deh wid yuh man.

Baps yuh tek taxi go look
Fi de bess obeah man
Him name is mass Fitzy
Ef anyting wrong 'im can fix it

Yuh no 'ave no clue
Mi 'ave one cousin name Sue
Anyting soun funny or look too blue
Noh go noh come she sware a duppy Jue.

Wen Jue was living, Sue neva like har
Because she was a man tief
An as yuh woulda imagine fi har man
Was one of de wild man eena districk.

Mi neva si a set a people believe eena obeah
So throw ice pan dem house top
Wen mawning light dem gaan ah obeah man
A look fi wah dem no pu' dung.

So mass Fitzy tek dem money
Bathe dem eena dutty wata
An mek dem drink dem own condemnation
Sell dem bottles of holy wata
An' wateva else dem want.

As mi granny woulda sey duppy know who fi frighten?

OLD TIME JAMAICAN COMMERCIALS AND REMEDY

Breeze washes so clean clothes even smell clean with breeze

Dragon Stout Put it Back

Smirnoff leaves you breathless

Milo Makes you go forever- tek dis one anyway yuh want, but it was some kind of a
runner pon de can. Dis can was used to store brown sugar after de Milo was finished

Fanta Soda go a town Denoes and Geddes, D& G lick him dung, Coke
co Cola pick him up carry him a Fanta fi fix him up, la,la,la, la

Best dressed Chicken in Town, now who coulda come up wid
such an idea fi put on clothes pan chicken fi eat.

Yes mi chile fi wi commercial back in de days were funny fi true. Who remember
Lactogen baby formula eena de blue an' white tin and Cowengate eena de orange
tin? Betty Milk verses Nestles condensed milk, Ovaltine rival Milo.

Andrews Liver Salts – Fi upset stomach

Bay Rum – fi bad feelings an' some people drink it

Canadian Healing Oil- fi pain an' bruises

Blue Stone – fi sore foot, it bun like peppa

Dettol- disinfectant for all purpose, for all skin cuts, in bathwater, use in laundry, mop
house fi smell fresh. Mixed wid dismatch bush for cuts from zinc a, barb wire an' nails

Gention Violet- for wounds

Jayse for serious infection especially on animals

Mercurior combe- reddish color for cuts an' bruises

Warm lamp oil fi colic belly ache wat a remedy, it wuk fi real

Anybaddy have headache, Phensic fi adult

Cafenol fi pickney fever an' pain

Gripe water fi baby belly ache

Scotts Emulsion fi build you up
Liquorfruta fi all colds, taste bad like some garlic mixture wid herbs
Ferrol Compound fi adults
Sulphur Bitters fi cleansing an' Massa it bitta fi true
Vicks vapor rub fi everything
Coconut Oil freshly made after yuh grater an' boil doung an' saka, saka, yuh finga knucle dem
Coconut oil use fi everything, cooking, fi yuh hair, fi yuh skin like lotion,
Miss Matty Cocnut oil now de pon top shelf, mi glad mi get enough
a it already. Yuh si fi yuhself country life was good livin'
Raw Cod-liver Oil wid a half orange on a Saturday morning or Serase Tea yuh know wat time it is
Band-Aid was called Elastoplast
Panadol fi monthly belly ache
Blue fi white clothes, Guinea gold, Magic, Blue, and brown soap fi wash clothes
Carbolic, Lifebuoy, Castile, Rexona, Palmolive, cashmere Bouquet for bathing
and Neko soap fi bumpy and Acne face, and ef yuh kno' smaddy a farin
yuh get Pear, Jergens, Ivory, Irish Spring and special Dove Soap.
Yuh ever wanda why Jamaican housewives mix dem own floor polish dem buy clear floor
polish Rexo or Cardinal, den buy Red Oak dye a market . I must sey dem wood floor shine
like a Dollar piece water bead off a dem and den afta yuh spen' Satuday all day pan fi yuh
knee wid de famous coconut brush an' claat only visitor was allowed fi walk pan dat floor.
Yuh memba dem specila plate glassware an' utensils just for visitors. Noh mine tings
diffrant now everbaddy a use disposable, nuhbaddy naah spen' dem evenin' a washup
plate an' scour pot wid coconut husk an' ashes. Mi countrygal still love de memories
of dem deh days. Ef yuh neva live it yuh miss a whole heapa yuh cultcha.

As mi granny woulda sey, yuh soon know weh wata walk goh a pumpkin belly

Bleaching Zinc Stand for White clothes, we never used chlorox bleach when I was a child in our household. The sunlight and soap water, any powdered laundry soap Fab, Breeze, Sudsil, Ajax, Tide or Magic, Guinea gold, blue or brown soap. Yes real coutrygal will remember this important piece of laundry equipment, whch is still used today. Dem clothes would be so white is was blinding. Then you would take them up, wash them out and rinse in blue water, before hanging on the line to dry. Yes those were the days of hand laundry.

As mi Granny woulda sey, nuh dash wey yuh stick before yuh cross river.

OLE HIGUE MUMMA

Ole higue, ol higue!? Ole higue mumma!
De pickney dem, dey halla' out
Tek time kibba yuh mout
For ole higue mumma will cuss yuh out.

Dem 'ave all right fi call har ole higue mumma
Wat a piece ah misery
De woman miserable like wen
Jackass kruppa no set right pan 'im,
Or wen hog eena harness.

But as pickney, it is de sweetest ting fi do
Halla out people nik name a hide dem backa bush.
A Noh ole higue mumma alone deh come,
Si two neck, dry foot Benji an' hipshotted Sue.
Wi mus prepare fi run for two neck,
Can throw rock stone roun' corna.

Dis is goin to be fun shhh quiet, her dem come
Oonu ready fi bawl out, an' run like mad.
One, two, tree, si dem yah
Biff, baff, buff, biddim, buddin, bap,
As wi tumble dung thru Mass Charlie caaffee walk.

As mi granny woulda sey,
A who de cap fit dem wear it.

OUT AH MANY ONE PEOPLE

Some ah oonu nowadays people would'n understan'
Wen wi sey Out Ah Many One People
African, Chinyman, Syrian, Indian, Jews, Gentiles, Italian,
Englishman, French, Spaniards, Conquistadores and our Native Arawak Indian
A really soh it goh.
For wi Mix up Jamaicans bruk all records
Dere is noh odda nation in de Worl' like wi
Talking bout colour, all shades of skin and yeye,
Wi unstoppable an' try anyting fi survive, hungry naah kill wi
Some people claim dem noh black dem is Jamaican
"cause dem did touch wid lickle English, an' as fi di chiney an' Indian dem eena class by dem self
Is only eena fi wi Islan' everybaddy gat dem owna Birt' Right.
Soh noh worry'bout yuh granpa ef him was an Englishman an' yuh granma was a Maroon,
All I want fi tell oonu is dat wi a nice people dat is most a wi
For 'mongst wi grace an' beauty some a wi need nuff pity, It noh matta wi color creed or ethnicity
Try yuh best noh tek noh liberty
Stir up Jamaican people an yuh wi know dem etiquette
Ramgutang, Zutopek, Sketel, Boogoyagga and oolum wi can be eena flash
Memba mi a tell yuh Edication, Religion or position don't stop
noh Jamaican from puttin' yuh eena yuh place
For Out Of Many One People.
As mi granny woulda sey;
Ef yuh noh mash ants, yuh noh know him belly or betta yet every pretty rose gat macka fi juk yuh.

PALISADOES AIRPORT TRIP

First it was a Marooned color Woolsey 1660 Motor car license plate number X 4388. This was a car I thought could not done. My dad's car was the car of the people. It made several trips to Spanish Town Registrar office to find Birth certificates and marriage documents for country people trying to find their way to England, Canada and United States of America. It was loaded with all the family on Sundays for church and we all fit in with no complain. The best trips were to the Palisadoes Airport later known as the Norman Manley International. This was outing at its best. People really got dressed up and brought cooked food with them to enjoy the whole day in the waving gallery. If you never had this experience, its hard to explain the excitement, anxiety and anticipation and beliefs that you really believe the person leaving could see you from that distance waving st them when they were already in the plane even at nights for those England flight. Those days life was sweet and people were much kinder and nicer, that's the Jamaica I longed for when we really said "No Problem Man" and meant it.

When Pan am, Lufthansa, eastern Airlines, British Airways and those navy blue travel bags with BOAC written on the side and if you ever got one of those bags you would show it off as if you were the person that traveled. People use to put down some bawling when people were leaving like the person had died. Well in fact some of them might as well dem fling rock stone backka dem an' yuh neva hear from dem again.

De best memory I recall wid airport trip was my dad took some children one night from Tranquility in Portland dem was going to England to dem madda an' dem granny spen' whole day frying fish, buy up duck bread, roast Captain Bligh breadfruit for dem England journey. Wen dad returned late dat night an' I went to meet him by de car to help wid anything needed to be carried into de house. Mi daer ma mi notice a lovely basket in de car trunk, wen mi open de basket noh de whole basket of de fry fish, yellow heart roast bread fruit and duck bread left just for Parson pickney dem. Up to tidday day wi call de findings Bancroft Bread an Fish, dat was de name of de lady grandson mi noh memba him siats dem name. Mi can still taste an' smell dat fish an' breadfruit.

As mi Granny woulda sey, wah drop offa head drop pan shoulda

PEASY HEAD BWOY

Miss Liza everybody want run fi politics
Some a dem don't know dem ayse from dem ass.
An de heep a gunshot mi de hear a night time
Cause mi fi a sleep undaneath mi bed ma.

Miss Matty peasy head bwoy
Weh graduate from university,
Decide im a run fi some office
I don't know why dat de bwoy
Wid de brains im gat neva tun
Doctor, lawyer or teacher.

Mi heart jus a gallop an'beat
Eena mi chess all day lang
Lakka wen bad dawg de chase smaddy.

Anyway mi hear seh im 'ave im own bodyguard,
Mi wish im good luck
Dem 'ave voting a mawning
Mi nuh wi si yuh den,
Me gaan before gunfire.

As mi granny woulda sey
Every sun-hot got im shady tree.

JAMAICAN ROADSIDE SHOES REPAIR MAN

POUND. F. SHILLINGS. S AND PENCE. D

Old fashion money Pound Shillings an' Pence, new money betta money is dollas an' cents, a memba dat commercial so well it was September 1969. My fada was one of de people chosen in de community to teach others how dis was gwine come about. It was fun fi us pickiney an' if youh come from Buff bay Portland yuh mus did know or hear of Rev. Hart an' his big family nine pickiney eight girls an one bwoy.

De people dem onc day came by de house an' left one of de biggest flat looking Dulcemenia grip, it was called de decimal currency grip. It contained all de information to covert yuh money from Pound Shillings and Pence to Dollas an' Cents. Wat a confusion it was fi de poor country people dem. Soh me an' mi bredda an' sistas got de fus lesson in dis money conversion.

It was fun to us for wi neva have any money fi convert. It was not easy fi most people at de time. Yuh memba dem deh days most people money eena pan unda bed mattress or hidden in places where they don't even memba for de one bank all de way in Buff Bay was too far fi have yuh money. Yuh si wen wi tek weh wiself from England it was only time before she demand har Pound Shillings and Pence.

An' some a wi really love de Royalty part so wi neva want fi leggo de King, Queen and all de odda Royalty face pan dem money.

But wat frighten me tiday is dat mi neva know de day woulda come wen Jamaicans refuse coin fi change, like dollar, five dollar an even twenty dollar. Wen dem mek five hundred dollar bill wid nanny face pan it mi did tink it woulda last fi ever den One Thousand Dollar bill came out wid Michael Manley face by de time yuh sey look ya it done like breeze blow it out a yuh hand. I memba clearly wen Jamaican twenty dollar bill was de largest note an' it took days before yuh could spend it off. Massa since Gilbert blow seems like everything get light from dem deh time. All I know keep hope rain a fall but dutty tuff, whedda yuh hav' Pound Shillings and Pence or Dollars an' Cents, by de time yuh get it, it done.

As mi Granny woulda sey, every mikkle, mek a mukkle.

RACE HORSE

Si de jackass a gallop down de
Back stretch wid all a
Mi rent money pan im
A weh mi deh go sleep tonight.

Mass Amos yuh tell mi
Dejackass blue magic was a sure winna
Mi tan up pan de side track
An all de yell me de yell an ride de jackass
'im gallop weh wid mi money same way.

De mawga jockey deh ride de jackass
Like 'im corn toe deh bun im
Or de jackass got chigga
Cold sweat a wash mi now.
An' dat is not all, mi belly de rumble to.

I don't know who got warra
But de whole a mi money
Gallop weh before mi very yai
Yuh know all de tings
I coulda do wid dat money.

No tek yuh money place pon
No jackass unless a yuh deh ride it.
So wen yuh loose yuh race
Yuh nuh 'ave nobaddy fi blame, but yuh self
Tek it from mi.

As mi granny woulda sey
Farden pocket an' poun a cheese.

SABINA PARK

Hurry up an' gallang eena de place
'cause mi naah miss one beat a disya cricket game yah tidday
yuh know how long mi ah wait fi a day like dis
A de fus time mi deh come a sabina fi watch cricket
Weh mek yuh buy demy a seat eena de sun hot.

Yuh tink mi need fi tan or a tingy yuh tingy star apple an' yuh mussa cousin.
Ku pan de heapa shady seat de people dem got
An'yuh got mi eena sunhot, ah it mek mi neva date yuh
Wen mi was much younger, but yuh know weh freeniss exist is folly to resist
For tidday mi is planning fi get mi moneys wort'
Mi nah lef till close of play an' dem pick up de wicket an' de bale.

Ah hope dem West Indian cricketer drink up dem Guinness an' dem Irish moss last night
For dem English man wi fine out tidday who is de bes eena cricket.
Mass Joe a weh dem deh wen wi use to play cricket wid young orange, grapefruit
an old golf ball an use coconut bow fi bat an' old rusty zinc fi wicket.
Si dem a come yah, lawks dem clothes white soh till
It a gi mi dark yeye, mi sorry sey mi neva borrow Miss Inez old darkers.

Yes lick de ball over mid wicket an' four boundary an' ever so often put one outa duppy gate
Yes wat a match up dat was dem West Indian bwoys show dem who is king
I cyant wait fi tomorrow, it a get dark come wi goh home.

As mi granny woulda sey
Learn fi dance a yaad before yuh goh abroad.

SKY HIGH

Everyting gaan up so high
But dem naah tap mi from
Tek mi airbus eena sky
Jamaica people don't care
A weh de money a come from
Dem mus reach 'merica
Fi buy dem pretty dan, dan.

Neva mine yuhself ya mah
Is mi fus trip trip to New York?
Mi hear sey dem 'ave
One big apple up deh
An' mi deh go look fi mi share.

Mi nuh care how much
People jam dem torpido teet'
Eena de apple aready
Piece mus lef fi mi.

So yuh step one side gi mi pass
Mi a go essin up mi self
An' put on mi make up,
New York, New York
Here I come.

As mi granny woulda sey
Come si mi an' live wid mi
A two diffrant tings.

SLOW DUNG

Slow dung yuh van massa
Yuh noh si de heep a wata,
A weh 'im come from doh een
De man si sey rain jus tap fall.

An 'im a drive like 'im noh si people
'im lucky 'im slow dung
For I an I a wait wid two rock
Stone eena mi han', fi get 'im attention

For any missa man who wet mi up
Tidday eena mi nice Clark shoes
I woulda teech 'im a lessen
Yuh can call it unforgettable.

Neva mine dat, yuh too materialistic
Mi jus no waan fi ketch no germs
Eena mi pretty face, or wet up mi hair piece
For dem noh cheap fi buy.

Sometime mi affi wanda to myself
Ef dem yah nowadays cyar people
Eva did walk foot,
Dem gallang like dem bawn wid
Steering weel eena dem han.'

As mi granny woulda sey
Neva si come si is a juice eva ting.

SORRY FI MAWGA DAWG

Nuh matta wah yu do fi some people I neva enuff
Yu coulda tek out yu heart an stuff ole claat eena
Yuh bossam dat nuh mek nuh diffarance
Mi dear chile mi tek miself an 'elp out smaddy
Weh day eena dem dilemma

De people dem decide fi tek mi on
Yuh woulda tink sey mi neva do nutten fi dem
From mi was bawn, 'ow dem carry on.
Dem galang wid one sinting mah
Dem bwile up an' steam
Is a good ting I was not gasoline
For de whole place woulda go up in hell flame
De way dem 'aul an' pull mi name.

I mek one wheel an go thru de gate
An all dem a cuss I nuh sey one wud
A memba wah mi granny tell mi
Wen yu bex nuh talk
Because ef mi did start fi trace
Nite woulda ketch up wid mi.

Mi pot a bikkle nearly bun up
Fi dem de people massa
It neva wort' mi time.

Is nuh wanda dem ole people seh
Sorry fi mawga dawg dem tun roun bite yuh.

STAY PUT

Ah noh everybaddy belong ah foreign
Some a oonu fi tan a yuh yaad
All dem do ah fi gi trouble abroad.
For it all start wen smaddy sen' dem
Invitation letta from "Merica.

Boops dem fine demself a Spanish Town birt' paper office
Wen dem jolly well know sey a yaad dem bawn
An'nobaddy neva regista dem birt'.
Yuh memba wen Miss Imogene tun-foot neice
Mumma lean –mout Kizzie chigga foot bwoy dah goh "merica.

All lakka him noh even fig oh a front yaad,neva mine tek plane ride Some people fi ween dem
mine offa foreign l Like how sun noh shine a night him know wen daylight Teng God dat
bruckup neva goh for him cyan scarcely help himself Mi know fi sure him was neva regista ah
Spanish Town Or noh weh else 'cause Imogene did 'ave soh mich a dem she loose count afta ten.

Neva mine yaah Aunt Girlie,mi know yuh wi miss de 'merican parcel dem Wid
de sweet smelling soap an sinting dem But kip heart cousin Sue, speaky spokey
nephew must bring back Sinting fi yuh, afta him tan soh long abroad.

As mi granny woulda sey
While breat'a blow fedda mus' grow.

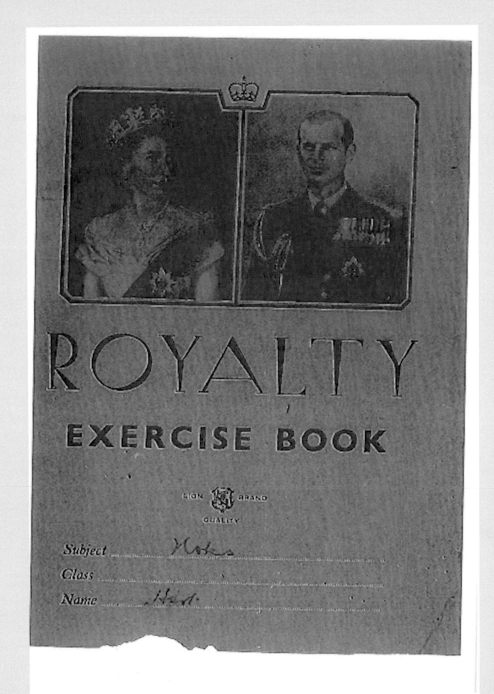

TEECHA TIME

Yes mi dear everybaddy
Mus know one big teecha
For wen mi yai was at mi knee
Big teecha beat mi fi laan ABC.

So nuh tell mi now thru yuh
Educated an matriculated
An know all dem big wuds deh
Yuh figet Miss Leachy School.

How could yuh? A de fus school
Yuh madda drap yuh off
Wen yuh neva know A from bull foot
An'de day yuh wet up yuh self.

But wait, a big school was de ting
Now fi meet Man Teecha
Him siddung a mawning time
Near school gate fi si all who de come late.

Nuh mek mi tell yuh
How ledda ban bun skin
Mi jus a wanda tidday day
Ongle to mi self, a who did gi im
De autority fi beat up pan smaddy.

Yuh woulda tink sey
A fi him pickney dem, shet up yuh mout'
It too late fi deh quarrel, ova spill milk
Tek time gwaan yuh ways.

Is a good ting appen fi yuh
Dem ya pickney nowadays
Need fi get de same medicine

As mi granny woulda sey
Nuh care how teecha cross,
School boun fi gi recess.

ARITHMETICAL TABLES

NUMERATION TABLE
Units 1
Tens 1 2
Hundreds 1 2 3
Thousands 1 2 3 4
Tens of Thousands ... 1 2 3 4 5
C. of Thousands 1 2 3 4 5 6
Millions 1 2 3 4 5 6 7
Tens of Millions 1 2 3 4 5 6 7 8
C. of Millions 1 2 3 4 5 6 7 8 9

STERLING MONEY TABLE
4 Farthings	1 Penny (d.)
12 Pence	1 Shilling (s.)
2 Shillings	1 Florin
2 Shillings & 6 pence	1 Half-Crown
5 Shillings	1 Crown
10 Shillings	1 Half Sov.
20 Shillings = 1 Sover.	1 Pound (£)
21 Shillings	1 Guinea

ARITHMETICAL SIGNS
+ Plus, Sign of Addition
− Minus, Sign of Subtraction
× Sign of Multiplication
÷ Sign of Division
= Sign of Equality
∷ Sign of Proportion
√ Sign of the Square Root
∛ Sign of the Cube Root
° ′ ″ Degree, Minute, Second
∴ Therefore

TROY WEIGHT — For Gold & Silver
24 Grains	1 Pennyweight (dwt.)
20 Pennyweights	1 Ounce (oz.)
12 Ounces	1 Pound (lb.)

APOTHECARIES' WEIGHT — For Mixing Medicines
20 Grains	1 Scruple (scr.)
3 Scruples	1 Drachm (dr.)
8 Drachms	1 Ounce (oz.)

AVOIRDUPOIS WEIGHT
For all Goods, except Gold, Silver and Jewels
16 Drams	1 Ounce .... (oz.)
16 Ounces	1 Pound .... (lb.)
14 Pounds	1 Stone .... (st.)
28 Pounds	1 Quarter .... (qr.)
4 Quarters	1 Hundredweight (cwt.)
20 Cwt.	1 Ton

HAY AND STRAW WEIGHT
36 lbs. Straw	1 Truss
56 lbs. Old Hay	1 Truss
60 lbs. New Hay	1 Truss
36 Trusses	1 Load

LONG OR LINEAR MEASURE
12 Lines	1 Inch .... (in.)
12 Inches ...	1 Foot .... (ft.)
3 Feet	1 Yard .... (yd.)
6 Feet	1 Fathom
5½ Yards	1 Pole
40 Poles	1 Furlong
8 Furlongs or 1760 Yards, 1 Mile

CLOTH MEASURE
2¼ Inches	1 Nail
4 Nails	Quarter of a Yard
4 Quarters	1 Yard

SOLID OR CUBIC MEASURE
1728 Cubic Inches ...	1 Cubic Foot
27 Cubic Feet	1 Cubic Yard
114 Cubic Feet	1 Ton
306 Cubic Feet	1 Rod of Brickwork

IMPERIAL LIQUID MEASURE
8 Gallons	1 Bushel
3 Bushels	1 Sack
12 Sacks	1 Chaldron

IMPERIAL DRY MEASURE
2 Glasses ...	1 Gill
4 Gills	1 Pint
2 Pints	1 Quart
4 Quarts	1 Gallon
2 Gallons ...	1 Peck
4 Pecks	1 Bushel
8 Bushels ...	1 Quarter

SQUARE MEASURE
144 Square Inches ..	1 Square Foot
9 Square Feet	1 Square Yard
30¼ Square Yards ..	1 Square Pole
40 Poles	1 Rood
4 Roods	1 Acre
640 Acres	1 Square Mile

TABLE OF MOTION
60 Seconds	1 Minute
60 Minutes	1 Degree
30 Degrees	1 Sign
12 Signs or 360°	the circle of the earth

TABLES OF TIME
60 Seconds	1 Minute
60 Minutes	1 Hour
24 Hours	1 Day
7 Days	1 Week
28 Days	1 Lunar Month
365 Days	1 Year
366 Days	1 Leap Year
52 Weeks	1 Year
12 Calendar	1 Year
13 Lunar Months	1 Year

Days in the Months
Thirty days hath September,
April, June and November;
All the rest have thirty-one,
Excepting February alone,
Which hath but twenty-eight days clear,
And twenty-nine in each leap year.

MULTIPLICATION TABLES

2 TIMES	3 TIMES	4 TIMES	5 TIMES	6 TIMES	7 TIMES	8 TIMES	9 TIMES	10 TIMES	11 TIMES	12 TIMES
1 are 2	1 are 3	1 are 4	1 are 5	1 are 6	1 are 7	1 are 8	1 are 9	1 are 10	1 are 11	1 are 12
2—4	2—6	2—8	2—10	2—12	2—14	2—16	2—18	2—20	2—22	2—24
3—6	3—9	3—12	3—15	3—18	3—21	3—24	3—27	3—30	3—33	3—36
4—8	4—12	4—16	4—20	4—24	4—28	4—32	4—36	4—40	4—44	4—48
5—10	5—15	5—20	5—25	5—30	5—35	5—40	5—45	5—50	5—55	5—60
6—12	6—18	6—24	6—30	6—36	6—42	6—48	6—54	6—60	6—66	6—72
7—14	7—21	7—28	7—35	7—42	7—49	7—56	7—63	7—70	7—77	7—84
8—16	8—24	8—32	8—40	8—48	8—56	8—64	8—72	8—80	8—88	8—96
9—18	9—27	9—36	9—45	9—54	9—63	9—72	9—81	9—90	9—99	9—108
10—20	10—30	10—40	10—50	10—60	10—70	10—80	10—90	10—100	10—110	10—120
11—22	11—33	11—44	11—55	11—66	11—77	11—88	11—99	11—110	11—121	11—132
12—24	12—36	12—48	12—60	12—72	12—84	12—96	12—108	12—120	12—132	12—144

John Dickinson & Co. Ltd. MADE IN GREAT BRITAIN London

TIME REALLY HAAD

Lawd Massa rain a fall but dutty tuff
Me ha six pickney an sence mi
Stop tek dem puppa to court
Mi is dem ongle bred winna.

Before sun can rise a mawning
Mi git up long before mi stop yawning
A wonda weh de next meal deh
I tink so haad a times, I cyan sey.

Mi wi haffi tun mi han an mek fashin
Two piece a wood out a door
Julie ketch up de fiya before mi knead de flour
Si piece a yam, coco, dashine an' banana.

Yuh tink a everybaddy 'ave chicken an steak
Wen white squawl tek charge a yuh
Tan deh a specify wah yuh waan fi nyam
Wen hungry a bus yuh shut an' rain a fall wen dutty tuff.

Borrow yuh sista shoes she deh complain
It too tight, she neva si people widdout feet
Get pan de platform an' recite wid all yuh might
For yuh mus bring home de prize money tonight.

Nobaddy eena de audience won't know
Sey a neda fi yuh shoes or frock or shoes
All dem need fi know is dat yuh a one
Of Rose dry foot pickney de judge dem choose.

As mi granny woulda sey
Wen trouble tek yuh pickney shut
Fit yuh.

TOO FAAS

Mek mi tell yu 'bout red yai nega
Dem no want fi si yu praspa
Before dem try fi fine out
'ow yu get yu sinting dem mek up
dem own story.

Tara day mi visit Sue
An shi start fi tell mi dat
Bev tell Finie how shi buy new cyaar,
An' nuhbaddy can bawl like shi
'bout how shi nuh gat money.

De 'usban fava heng pon nail
Wen 'im tink sey 'im well dress
Fi dem mirra mus be upside dung
No badda mention de pickney
Dem ah advertisement fi ole bruck.

Missis mi nuh know weh mek
Shi tink shi afi keep up wid de Jones
Wen dem nuh 'ave wah fi nyam or wear
But dem 'ave new cyaar.

Any ways mi nah faas eena backra bizniz
Fi mi own a pwile and mi man out fi lef mi
'cause mi walk a road too much an a gossip
mi gaan ya mah
se-yuh eena de morrows, same place same time.

As mi granny would a sey
tung double bring whole heap a trouble.

TOO MUCH BIZNIZ

I want fi know who de go buy,
Because everyone gat sinting fi sell.
From I bawn till now
Or from independence of 1962.

I neva witness so much people a sell,
Higlering tun big bizniz.
Everybaddy gat sinting fi sell
Yuh from foreign.

Yuh know Jamaica boast a wedda
Of eighty five degrees all year roun.
Imagine yuh can get lang ledda boots
Up to yuh high tigh, fur coat, gloves an' scarf fi match.

Fi mi Jamaican people will sell,
Any an everyting because
Smaddy de fi buy at all times.

I pass my place an' go ax a peddler,
Why all these winta tings
Shi look pan mi awful strange
An ax mi sey if I neva hear
Of de Jamaica Bobsled Team.

As mi granny woulda sey
One, one coco full baskit.

JAMAICAN BANGARANG, MISS MATTIE LOU COLLECTION

88

TRAFFIC LIGHT

It is about time dem put up one
Stop light eena country,
Dem tink sey a ongle town people
Waan fi know wen fi go, pause or stop brap.

Mi always wonda wah politician tek country people fah
Dem tink sey ef fi wi vote noh count,
Yuh know how much people, pickney and dawg
Get lick dung an' kill eena cross road yah.

Yuh memba Dinah stamma bwoy wingy
Him tek so long fi de wuds fi cum out a him mout,
A it mek mas Ivan lick him dung wid im fitz wheel bicycle
An' gi him one helleba coco.

Dat day Massa was one commotion
Yuh couldn tell a who lick dung who
For de two a dem sprawl out eena de road speechless
Dem nearly mek dummy talk.

One snocone man did closeby
So smaddy beg him lickle sweet syrup
Fi gi dem a drink, yuh know fi revive
Dem from de shock.

Hear Miss Dinah stamma bwoy
Ooonnuu nuh, nuh 'ave noh spice bun
Everybaddy bus out a laugh
Yuh woulda tink a circus.

As mi granny woulda sey
Humpty dumpty neva fall dung offa noh wall
A smaddy shub him off.

TRAMCYAR RIDE TO MINI BUS

Miss Inez I neva tink de day woulda come, wen mi poor gal woulda miss clickety clung

Dat is de way tramcyar run, as it crawl thru de mawning sun

Miss Kitty dawg a bark like him noh si she day da light

Tap gal wha wrong wid yuh, is weh yuh deh blow so haad fa

Yuh noh si sey a seven 'a clack an' de tramcyar noh ketch a king rock yet

Missis stan study an kip heart, yuh know sey day long an time short

Lawks wat a cool breeze tek two deep breth an set yuh mine at ease

See it deh jus a bruk de corna, wen it tap get pan it an ole tight

For noh matta howyuh good yuh heart a dead wid fright

Mi did tink de tramcyar ride was bad, till mi tek de new minibus

Dem drive off before yuh siddung, an twenty-five a wi pak up like brunwick sardines eena can

Stick a pin, dem minibus mek fi cyaah fifteen people, noh mek mi tell how it fit twenty five a wi

An yuh dere not open yuh mout for de conucta will eat yuh live

So noh mek nobaddy tell yuh bout modern transportation

Tek it from mi slow an' steady win de race, wi soon reach for mi blood pressure a rise

pon every corner him tek, do mek wi come off a de next stop mi wi walk de rest.

As mi granny woulda sey

New broom sweep clean, but old broom know de corna.

WEN YUH LAN

Jamaica people bole mi chile
Jamaica people gran
Dem nuh easy at all
Weh eva dem go
People 'ave de juice fi understan.

Dem get pon top and Massa
Gi dem a inch
De whole yaad a fi dem
An' dem done de mile.

So wen yuh lan' eena forein place
An white man wid him deep blue yai
Ax yuh face to face
Is weh yuh cum from?
Clear yuh troat an' get yuh speech togedda.

Well dem mek de bes' white rum deh
De beaches are very beautiful an famous
Tell him bauxite, jerk pork
An' de famous Blue Mountain coffee.

An' wen yuh lef deh, dis mawning
De sun neva rise yet
But a da lickle islant dem call Jamaica

A deh mi com from,
Anymore question sah?

Because mi know sey, before yuh twang
All a dat eena patois
De poor ting will 'ave de juice fi understan.

As mi granny seh
Wen dish towel tun table claat
Is nuttin' but a pess to de table.

TRIBUTE TO MY MENTOR POEM BY MISS LOUISE BENNETT

Jamaican society is sometimes said to be conditioned to preachments- religious and secular. Every man is a parson under the skin. The religious tradition has thrown up deacons and revivalist a – plenty. In this poem "me son Uriah" is able to pinch-hit at a moments notice, for the absent cletic.

Fe me fambly is not peaw-peaw,
Me daughta Sue da-teach.
An wen rain fall, or Parson sick,
Me son Uriah preach!

Sunday gone, rain come so till Parson
Could'n lef him yard,
People was 'eena church an so
Uriah get weh broad;

Him climb up pon di pulpit, him
Lean over, him look dung,
Him look pon all we enemy
An lash dem wid him tongue!

De fus one him tek on, was Lize
Who tell di lie pon me,
Him stare in a her face an say,
*'Thou art de mouti-mouti!'

**Him sey "Thou art de rowasam!"
"Thou art de meddlesam!"
An den him look pon me an sey,
**Thou art de slaughtered lamb!"

Him teck on Teacher Brown, for wen
Him was de size o' dat,
Teacher beat him one day because
Him call Teacher "top knot".

So 'Riah get him revenge now
For him stare straight pon Brown
An say, "let him dat sittet' on
De house-top not come down!"

Him teck on Butcher Jones, who noted
Fe sell scrapses meat,
Him say "Thou shalt not give thy neighbours
Floolooloops to eat!"

Him tell dem off, dem know is dem,
Dem heart full to de brim,
But as 'Riah eena pulpit
Dem can't back answer him!

So wen church membet mel me, I
Don't answer till it reach
A rainy-day wen Parson stay
Home, an Uriah preach.

PATOIS GLOSSARY

The inspired work of Janice Hart, "Miss Matty Lou" tells the rich stories of everyday Jamaica country life along with her personal experiences of growing up in the Parish of Portland. Miss Hart refers to herself as the Portland Countrygal. Readers who are interested in details of etymology, pronunciation, grammar and vocabulary of the Jamaican dialect will find Prof. Cassidy's book a rewarding and readable reference. The following list of words is therefore limited strictly to use as an aid in comprehending some of these poems. Miss Mattty Lou wants the reader to understand that "patois" words are spoken with differences in all fourteen parishes in Jamaica. The sounds and flow of the Jamaican Patois has been captivating audiences from all over the world for decades.

Aataclaps. Calamity, catastrophe, plenty trouble, chaos
A or ah. Is as in the alphabet A
Ali-button. Usually referring to someone who gets abuse working for nothing
Anting. Used as a descriptive word in addition. Three piece suit Anting.
Aringe. Orange the fruit or the color
Atta. After
Ayse. Ear
Ax or aks. Ask

Babylon. This word means oppression to Jamaicans, it's often used in the Rastafarian culture poetry and songs
Backside. The posterior of someone.
Backa. Behind
Backitive. Someone who has your back
Backra. White man, person of privilege, person in authority
Backa. Behind
Back whe. Too close to someone or something, give me distance.

Baffan. Awkward person especially with their hands, sewing, cooking, cleaning of fixing something simple

Badda. To bother someone

Baganpan. Your own belongings in excess

Bangarang. Worthless, good-for-nothing

Bans o'. A lot of

Barrah. Borrow

Bawl. As in cry.

Bex. Vex, irate, upset

Bikkle. Cooked food

Big-gill. Quarter of a pint

Biskit. Biscuit, a crackers

Boogooyagga. Not attired nicely and or personality is poor.

Boonoonoonus. Looking beautiful well-dressed or groomed. Nice and lovely a compliment.

Bokkle. Bottle

Bolo job. Hard work

Bongo, bungo. Black and ugly

Bredda. Bra, bro. Brother

Buck-buck. Large, forehead

Bulla. Cake made from flour, wet sugar and drinking soda

Butta. Butter

Brap. A sudden stop in a car or a conversation ending abruptly

Bruk. As in have no money broke

Boun'. Must as in getting recess

Bwile. Boil as to cook

Bwoy. Boy

Caaffee. Coffee

Capras. Copper container for boiling sugar

Chamba – Chamba . Disfigured

Chaka-chaka. Untidy not neat
Chichi-bud. Long-tail bird
Chi-chi-bus. Public transport buses with doors opened by compressed air, old Jolly Bus .J.O.S
Chigga. Fungus of feet especially toes.
Chigarookoo. Person infested with chigoe
Cho. Interjection showing impatience, skepticism or mild scorn-almost like English
Cirosee or cerasee. Vine, bitter in taste, used for medicinal purposes
Claat. Cloth
Combolo. Friend companion
Coub or coob. Fowl house
Counta or 'count '. On account of
Cowl. Cold
Crismus. Christmas
Crommoogin. Selfish, self-centered

Dan. Than
Darkers. Sunglasses
Dawg. Dog
De. The
Deggeh or deggeh. Sole, only
Deh. There
Deh-deh or did-deh is there
Dem. Them
Dess. As in despeartion
Destant. Decen
Dinna. Dinner
Dip. To be deported to one's country
Diss. To show disrespect
Disya . This here
Doan. Don't
Dress-up. Dolled up

Drop-pan. Chinese gambling gamenamed from method of play
Duckoorioo. Pudding made from green banana leaves
Dung. Down
Duppy. Ghost
Duppy-conquera. Bully, (lit. conqueror of a ghost)
Dutty-dutty. Mud, muddy
Dweet. Do it

Eena. Into
Ef. If
Efa. If I
Eida. Either
Enkle. Ankle

Faba, fava. Resemble, favour
Facety. Impertinent, rude
Fah. For
Famelia. Familiar
Farden. Farthing
Farin. Foreign
Faas. As in speed or being nosy
Fava. Resemble or doing someone a favor
Fi. For
Figga. Figure out
Finga. Finger
Fi-mi. Mine
Fi mi own. My own
Fi we. Ours
Fenky-fenky. Ordinary, puny
Frase. Phrase

Gal. as in girl or a measure gallon

Galang. Go along, leave

Gi. Give

Gizzada. A sweet tart made with sweet spice grated coconut baked in a flour pastry opened

Goh. Go as to go, leave

Gran'. As in grand market

Gwan. Go on

Gwine. Going to, the store or to speak

Haffi. Have to

Hag. As in a pig.

Haggler. Peddler, a street seller

Halla. Call out loud

Han-miggle. Palm of hand

Helleba. Describing something large/ big

Helleba coco. Knot on one's head caused from a blow to head.

Heng. Hang as in clothes on line, nail or hanger

Hipshotted. Unstable gate in walking in pain at all time

Histry. History

Hooda really. Would really, or would have really

Hooden. Wouldn't

Ile. Oil

Jerk-pork. Seasoned pork cooked by steaming under the earth

Katta. A head piece usually made from dried banana leaves or cloth, placed on one's head to carry load, especially baskets by market vendors. (Higglers)

Ketch. Catch

Kyah. Carry

Kyar. Car

Kibba. Cover
Kip. Keep
Koo. Look
Koo yah. Look here, take notice
Kruppa. A donkeys padding used to steady load on donkeys back
Kutty Kap. The sound of donkey or horse hoofs

Lakka. Like comparison looks like
Laan. As to learn a lesson
Lawd. Lord
Liard. Liar, lying
Lidung. Lie down

Macka. Thorns as in roses
Malatta. Mulatto, half-caste
Manasable. Polite
Mass. Mister as in "Mass Burtie"
Mawning. Morning
Mawga. Meagre, skinny
Mell. Trouble, or to bother someone
Memba. As in member of an organization or to remember something
Mo. More
Mout-a-massi. Someone who talks about others at all times chatter-box
Mouty-mouty. A very talkative person
Mus-mus. Mouse, mice
Mussa. Must be

Naasy- naasy. Untidy person
Naa. Not
Naaga. Negro; describing a behavior

Naily. Nearly
Nie-nite. Wake held for nine nights after the death of someone.
Ninyam. Food
Nize. Noise
Nooh. No
Noh. Not
Nuh. Not, no
Nuff. As in plenty
Nutten. Nothing
Nyam. Ea

Odda. Other
Offa. Off
Ole. Old
Oonoo. You (plural)
Omuch. How much as in cost or how old are you?
Ongle. Only
Outa – outside
Ovah. Over, finish
Owna- man. A person who owns car, property or anything else

Pantomine. Pantomime, annual Jamaican Musical
Patty. Jamaica meat pie, I would describe the Jamaican Hamburger
Pawn. Hold firmly. Someone holding you very firm.
Peeny-wally. Big firefly with shining eyes usually seen at night especially in the countryside.
Peaw-peaw or pyaw-pyaw. Weak,
Feeble, ineffective
Fenky- Fenky—feeble usually referring to a person statue
Perangles or parangles. Problems, troubles, affairs
Pickney. Child
Pooh, poo. Poor

Pose. Suppose

Pu dung. Put down

Puppa or pupa. Father, papa

Pwile. Spoil

Quashie. Poor man, socially awkward person

Quatty. I ½ d.

Ramp. To play as in recess time or child's play

Run-dung. A meal usually pickled mackerel cooked with coconut milk

Saaf drinks. Carbonated drinks, soft drinks, sodas

Samfie. A trickster as in a con-artist

Sence. Since

Sey. Say

Sey-Sey. A talkative person getting in trouble wit others.

Seh. Say

Shet. To close, lock. Shet de door

Shetpan. A closed container used to store and carry food, usually leftovers

Siddung. Sit down

Sinting. Something

Slam-bam. Closing something final argument or sometimes a door

Slap- dash. A job not done well (Sloppy)

Smaddy. Somebody. A person

Soon-a-morning. Early in the morning

Soon- come. Not necessarily in a hurry or even the same day

Solja. Soldier

Splendashus. Splendid nicely put together

Stingy or tingy. Frugal person

Su-su. Gossip a lot

Surrup. Syrup used for snow-cones,

Tallawah. Stalwart male

Tan. Stand, stay

Tan tudy. Stand still

Tarra. That there

Teggereg. Bully or too bossy

Tenk or tenky. Thanks

Tickya. Take care that

Tidday. Today

Tadda. The other person or the day of the week.

Togedda. Together

Tudy. Steady / Study

Tup. Relating to old British money used prior 1969 also used to describe quantity.

Tung. Town, downtown Kingston

Twang. Accent in speaking like a British or American

Unda. Under

Wat day. The other day, that day past

Wat lef. Usually referring to leftover food

Wi. We

Weh or wey. Where, way or away

Wha-fe-do. What to do!

Whai! Interjection to denote fright, despair

Who-fa. Belonging who owns

Wingy Peaw- Peaw. As in small in stature, fragile

Wud. Word

Wus. Worse

Wussa. Very bad (lit. worser)

Wusserer. Very, very bad (lit. worserer)

Wut. Worth

Yai. Eye

POEMS FROM THE SOUL

I Am So Glad You Came This Poem specially dedicated
to Mr. Harry Belafonte- by Janice M. Hart

I am so glad you came to the Motherland called Africa
Robbed me of my dignity and Humanity
Stripped me from wombs of Naomi and, Aku, ripped me from
the loins of Kenta Kente, Kwasi and Cudjoe
Raped my mothers, sisters and daughters, left my children orphans
Packed us in boats like sardines, pillarded us, and yanked us dragged us across the transatlantic sea
But I am so glad you came
The tears of my forefather have watered the earth
In complete anguish and sorrow, they were left with unanswered questions this day.
The unborn in the wombs of salami, Aku and Naomi wept at the sounds of evil,
This cold journey of sure death for some of us, pain, sorrow, starvation and misery,
we arrived in the so called land of the Free and the home of the Slave.
We were placed on auction blocks in the boiling sun and sold for three fifths of a man.
Placed on cotton fields, tobacco field in the south and, sugar plantation in the Caribbean
But I am so glad you came to the Motherland called Africa
If you never came we would have never known
Alain LeRoy Locke, Thurgood Marshall, Dr. Martin Luther King Jr, Paul Roberson,
Langston Hughes, James W. Johnson, Claude McKay, Rosa Parks, Mary Bethune
McLeod, Benjamin Banneker, Lewis H. Latimer, W.E.B. DuBois, Marcus
Mosiah Garvey, Robert Nester Marley, Sidney Poitier, Mayo Angelou.
America's First Black President Barack Hussain Obama.
But only if you knew five hundred years later in the loins of Harold George and
Mary Belafonte, there lie a seed Harry George Belafonte Jr. born March 1, 1927, The

Civil Rights Activist, Performing Artist, Singer, Song Writer, Philanthropist. The
Gate Keeper of Justice and voice of Sankofa, you would have left me there.
I am so glad you came,

ALLEY CAT

Drug dealers, addicts, prostitutes, murderers if only the alley cat could talk.
Unidentified bodies, abandon children, runaways, babies wrapped in trash bags left to die.
Crack phials, heroine needles and syringes, crack pipes used condoms,
clothes strewn everywhere this is home for me and many others.
It use to be very peaceful once upon a time.
Restaurants would dump their garbage back here, other cats and dogs would fight for the best
refuse that was fun. Now they are all gone, some ran away others killed by stray bullets.
Now my alley is infested with unsolved mysteries. I wish I could talk. I have
survived a few near death experiences myself and have one life left from
my nine. I am moving to a new alley hoping they won't find me.
Since I have lived in alleys most of my life my friends will always find me.
I am a real person.

ALMOST

And so I move on, like a wounded panther.
Moving stealthily across the desert floor, having lost it all.
I thought, only to realize I'm still breathing.
My predators in awe and shock, as if they were standing in an avalanche
Deeply hurt and severely wounded,
I pick up the broken pieces of my heart, or soul whichever.
Totally devastated I move on.

A SOLDIERS TALE

After the wars my nightmares would not go away
They were ever so real
The faces of anguish
The screams of death
The fowl smell of rotten flesh
And yes the mangled bodies
Arms that seems to reach out from beyond to grab me
Knowing that they were not attached to a body made me cringe.
We were all young innocent men not old enough to have a beer
The sounds of cannons and grenades exploding all around me as if
I had a permanent echo in my head.
A light rain began to fall as if the moon cried or God cried
To see the eminent destruction of young lives.
We jumped a shore as if we knew the geography of the land
And all hell broke loose, as explosion filled the air.
What chaos and confusion
In a distance I saw my friend Ted
As if he was buried in the sand to his chest and I wondered
For a minute why he was not coming nor was he waiting for me
When I got closer I realized his intestines were blown apart,
And he was dead. Damn those bastards I muttered what enemies?
My stomach turned as my breakfast was wretched from my guts.
My eyes welted with tears as I walked away from Ted.
I closed his eyes gently with my bloody fingers
And softly bid him goodbye.

Now this is war I said, I continued through Death Valley
And bloody gorges killing all enemy in sight near and far off
I said I must fight to the end for all my buddies who did not make it home.
Despair and cynicism swirl around in our minds
Like confetti on a windy new year's Day
Personally I don't care what anyone thinks these are awful times
Poverty is everywhere there is hardness in people's faces
Children wear scars of abuse, and orphanage they have forgotten how to laugh.
Everyone seems cold and shrugs their shoulders to say hello.
Soldiers are homeless and bear the permanent wounds of war.
They carry their earthly belongings in a shopping cart and sleep under bridges
And card board boxes, amazing they can survive this is hell
Our souls are leaking as I lay here beneath my tombstone Unknown Soldier.

ALONG THE RIVER BANKS

As I walked along the river banks
I felt the sun as it sneaked through
The trees above and embraced me
With its ultraviolet rays,
Such sensation of warm love.

As I heard the birds singing me a
A soft lullaby in the distance
They caressed my ossicles like
Snowflakes falling down my neck
On a warm summers evening.

Its then I noticed the leaves
As they danced to the music of the wind
Like young unicorns
Skipping on a beautiful spring day.

Then the river rushed by the banks
As it clap its hands for joy
Against the limestone rocks,
Yes, even the glory of nature
Praises the creator
In joy, peace and love.

AS GOD CRIED

The play ground was bare as the swing sets swayed in the
wind the echo of children's laughter was silent,
The cries of death already in the grave
The graves are not full yet, A war grew deeper in my heart
the anticipation of sure death was agonizing,
As we huddled in deafening silence
Our eyes screamed with fear,
Our hearts pounded the bony chest wall of our rib cage
As if it wanted to leap for freedom,
The smell of death and horror permeated the air
I never had the chance to think before or did I,
The church was riddled with bullets as the Virgin Mary statue gazed in
horror the floor screamed with the blood stains of my brothers and sister,
This was living hell or was it when I had to make friend with God,
That was surreal a moment

They never found me, but I found myself,
I prayed until I found peace
I learned how to love through the deepest and darkest moments of hate and pain,
My soul ached for the bloodshed of my people
The sun hid her face from the rain clouds,
As God cried....

AS DAWN BREAKS

As dawn breaks slowly into daylight
And fog seeps outside my windowpane
The dewdrops on every petal at morn
A garden still asleep awaiting daylight.

Wake up Wise Ocean in all your innocence
Welcome the fishermen at the break of dawn
Your silk sheets are now ruffled
Ships are sailing on your endless tides.

Oh mighty wind that comes blowing all day long
Whistle to me a song,
Where have you been hiding?
Above the trees so high or in the valleys so low.

Sunburst so orange and bright
Cast off your shadow of the night
My body still dragging behind
I must nurture these new thoughts in my mind.

"AWKWARD"

I wish I knew you mother.
It must have been an awful decision you made to give me
Away.
I cannot imagine the pain, the grief or the joy!!
I often thought of finding you, but my thoughts are; do you
Want to know me?
I have been well taken care of and loved now that I am
Thirty something years old and have children of my own.
There is still nothing closer than blood.
Are you satisfied with your life and have you moved on?
Can a mother's tender care cease towards the child she
Bears?
Maybe I should dismiss my thought and feeling.
Oh what void I feel.
I wish I knew you mother.

BEHIND IN MEMORIES

I am embarking on a new pathway in life
I am taking a trip in peace and harmony
I am leaving all my troubles behind
I must move on.

So goodbye to loneliness and heartaches

Goodbye to disappointments and despair,
Goodbye to depression and frustrations
I must move on and get out of here.

Hello to joy and happiness
What new peace I found in me,
It's so nice to dream just like an innocent child
I must move on my mind is at ease.

I will skip like a young lamb
On a beautiful summer day
And watch the butterflies as they flutter away,
I am moving on as the smell of blossoms fills the air.

I left all my troubles behind
Don't remind me about any of them,
If you happen to see them, leave them alone
I have moved on, come see my new world.

DON'T COME HERE

Grown men weep, boys are confused all hoping to wake up from this nightmare.
This is real a prison. If only I had time to think this over, I would not be here.
Prisons were not made for dogs, they are right no dog want to come here.
Dogs love their freedom too much,so why men chose to go there.
One hot tempered decision to rob, to rape, to kill, to sell drugs, to be an accomplice
to a crime, espionage whatever the crime may have been you must pay.
Every country and state have their laws and rules, violate them, you pay the consequence.

Doors slam, you are locked in, you are no longer the same. Life has becomes routine when to eat, bathe, exercise and use the bathroom are now dictated to you. You have become institutionalized, all your freedom was gone in a split second this is life behind bars. Minutes become hours, days, weeks, months, years a lifetime this is frightening. I am only twenty years old. What bleak future I carved for myself.
I am warning all my friends please don't come here.
Think long and hard before you act. Stay away from bad company.
Live the life for me that I gave away stupidly.
Parents tell your children especially your sons, street life does not pay.

DON'T LIVE IN THE PAST

Don't be angry about life's changes
The wind blows to the East and takes whatever is in its path.
Sometimes we standstill in life
And some spirit comes along and moves us.
Out of our comfort zone we go,
Uprooting and replanting is great for life's progress and purpose

Don't be angry about life's changes
You can sit here on this here plantation for the rest of your life
I will not let my pride keep me trapped
I am fuelled with excess passion that drives me
To seek freedom beyond these fences.
Imaginary fences are devastating.

Don't be angry about life's changes
In the stillness of this silver moonlight night my thoughts are awakened.
My passion for freedom as trickled down through my brothers and sisters

And the contagious factor is at work
So massah by daybreak there will be twenty less minds for you to worry about,
The winds blew East and life's process and progress changed instantly
So when all fails stand in the direction of the wind.

DON'T TAKE ME THERE

Don't take me down old memory lane
Where old men dressed in rags
Sit on street corners
With bottles in brown paper bags
Talking junk and playing card games
Hoping to win from the greatest loser
His dreams, aspirations and a life he yearned for.
Don't take me there
Down memory lane where hookers play tricks
And pimps stand by to beat their bitches
Where bullets fly as drug deals go awry
And gunmen do drive by.
Where hungry dogs park in the park
And children are afraid to play
'Cause there is no safe place to stay
Where ditches are full of death wishes
Don't take me there those days are dismal and dark
I have seen too much for a child to endure
Those sleepless nights when I listened
Death cries, fists thumping, swear words screaming,
So degrading is that living?
Will this violence creep underneath my door?

And enter my safe place.
Yes one night it did,
I am torn with such indelible bitter memories
That has scarred me for life.
Though battered, perplexed, dreams shattered and wounded
I have moved on.
Come see my new life.
Don't take me there down memory lane.

DOWNTOWN NEW HAVEN

What a people.
What an event.
What a mix of culture.
New Haven streets so dead and doom, bursting at its seams with talented contestants.
Some professionals, some amateurs, who cares who they are, people united for a worthy cause.
Yale University, which sits smack in the middle of downtown for the last three
hundred years, has kept this city culture alive and well. It is sometimes mind
boggling to know of the art and culture that is credited to this small town.
Black, White, Yellow, Pink, Blue, Green, people of all colors, creeds and race,
gather on the green with one goal in mind, to be entertained. Their geographical
location is irrelevant, they each have a big smile on their face.
The children are having a ball. This is unity at its best.
So all of New Haven natives who ran away from a city so rich in culture and
history, it is quite obvious you have no idea what you left behind.
Please return at least once a year every summer to enjoy our free concerts on the green.
Take my word these talents will make you scream.

<u>*EQUAL*</u>

Cry

Pain

Laughter

Birth

Health

Sickness

Wealth

Misfortunes

Marriages

Divorces

Death

We are all equal.

ETHNIC CLEANSING

The cries of babies were heard for years
Where was the rest of the world?
What horror
Unimaginable torture and pain
What crimes of war?
What ethnic cleansing?
Did Hitler and his men do enough?
Who is unclean?
Why did GOD really create mankind?
Unsightly remains of human skeletons everywhere you look.
Faces of humans all unknowns to the rest of the world it seems.
Once fathers, mothers, brothers, sister's babies and children.
What went so wrong?
For the ego of one man
To rid his world of people who were different.
God created us all different
That's the way he wanted it to be.
Who gave you the power to cleanse?
I can still hear the children cries.

GO BACK WHERE?

I never quite understood that
You brought me here I thought because you cared
You preached love and peace and blessings on our lives
Then got us to your shores and then we realized
We have been doped, bamboozled and tricked
You never painted pain or agony
I cannot tell where this journey will end
But I am damn sure where it begun.
A dark cold night as the waves battered the doors
Shivering and starving we were shackled to the ships
Human cargos unwilling to go
Some of us dying of starvation or from a shocking head blow
I think I am caught up in a dream that won't quit
Its seems dark as hell or the most bottomless pit
They tell me I am too young to understand
You must be kidding what is there to differentiate
The shackles that have cut to bones of my shin or the sever lashes to the black of my skin
You seem to be working on your human experiment
At all these Negroes expense
So wake me up when it's all over as my ancestors welcome me on the other side

Death before dishonor my dear.

IF YOU WERE DYING

Oh the things you would do if you were dying
You would be much kinder
You would laugh a lot more and be so happy
The petty things would pass you by
All caterpillars would be your butterfly
You would be more forgiving and be apologetic
You would love the people around you more
And would not care what people had to say
You would take long walks in the park with someone you love
If you knew you were dying
Listen to the birds as they serenade you with their melodies from above.
Enjoy the sunrises as well as the sunsets
Embrace the sunny days along with the cloudy ones.
You would do all the things in life that you wanted to do.
You probably go sky diving, bungee jumping, mountain climbing,
Or take yourself on a long Caribbean cruise
You would be much sweeter and gentler too
If you knew you were dying
So why don't you live everyday like you were dying
And be as sweet as fresh dew drops on rose petals
Soft snowflakes against your window pane
And tantalizing as dark chocolate on Valentine's Day.

I'M DONE PICKING COTTON

You see Massa I'm done picking cotton on your farm.
I am tired of bending over all day in that boiling sun,
Picking bales of cotton
That's just not my style these days.
I am an old slave not retired just over worked
I'm not crazy yet, although I could go crazy
Sitting here in my old rocking chair on my verandah doing nothing.
But it's my time now they tell me to enjoy life.
What life I asked them?
I can hardly see where I am going,
I can barely hear what you are saying
My body aches with pain they call arthritis.
And I should be enjoying life.
I was robbed of such privileges seventy plus years ago.
I made the great mistake and was born into slavery
Although my father was the plantation owner
I was considered to be a crossbreed; still a slave
I got no special treatment.
I picked cotton until my hands were blistered
My back and neck hurt severely from repetitious movements.
It was non-stop for every second of every minute of every hour
Of every day for sixty long years.
Slaves must be ubiquitous, in the midst of all that life
I found time for a family, a husband that I never officially married
And four children I never spent time with to teach

The basics about life, like ABCs, Nursery Rhymes
Old time stories about their ancestors and even fun times on moonlight nights.
Instead they learned how to pick cotton real soon.
So please don't tell me how to enjoy my life
I just want to sit here and relax with my favorite book
And don't forget my homemade lemonade.
Just leave me in this here rocking chair
With the gentle summer breeze and the warm sunrays on my olive face
'Cause old don't mean dead
Go on now my child
I have got work to do.

I QUIT YESTERDAY

I used to blame everyone for my pitfalls on Crack Street.
As I took my daily stroll at midday
This could not be my fault
You left it in my way.
I stopped again at the same place on Crack Street today
I stumble and fell in the same hole, I could not see
And I am certain I did not put it there
I fell in that same hole yesterday or am I imagining things
Or maybe I am in complete denial
Today I feel empowered
I have come to grips or my senses not sure
All I know, I have been here before, maybe one hundred times at least
But this time it feels real
I refuse to walk down Crack Street today
I am tired of blaming everyone else except, me
Today I am walking down Quit Street.
I Quit.

JUST WORDS

And long after time has passed or life is over,
The spoken word will go on forever.
They will echo in the rushing wind, the raging rivers,
The stillness of the dark nights.
In the twinkling of every star great or small,
The singing of birds on yonder hill far away.
The word will echo loud and clear,
When all the oceans kiss the shores.
When the winds caress the trees,
In the sun that shines, the plants will dance.
The brooks and springs will clap their hands for joy,
To the sound of words when we speak no more.
The planets will perform like a well-rehearsed celestial orchestra,
To the sound of words, we hear no more.
The words of Joy, Peace, happiness, knowledge, pain, laughter and sorrow, life and yes even death,
Were left by those who came before, but roam this earth no more.
We have the choice of words, to impact other fellowmen lives,
And yes long after I am gone you will be reading these words.
Words of an unsung poet,

Just Words.

LONGING

How I yearn to be home, just to listen to the
Roosters crow in the wee of the mornings.
Sometimes too early being fooled by the moonlight.
To see old farmers with their bags on their donkeys
In the dew of the morning going to the fields.
Yes the dogs barking, clinking and clanking of carts
And buckets getting water from the tanks.
To appreciate real people, the ones who stop to say
Good morning and to ask how are you feeling today?
Children skipping merrily along to school some
Barefooted, others with shoes, it really doesn't matter
They are happy.
Happiness that's what really counts, a state of mind.
How I long to go home.

LOOKING BACK

I have returned to visit these sixteen acres, hallowed ground
Now seems so innocent and naïve yet extremely haunting memories.
Memories though sparse is forever etched in my mind
Like the faces on Mount Rushmore.
I have ran away from my past before and even have buried ugly hatchets
But as crazy as it seems 911 is indelible.
I cannot put it at rest.

Because every moment it gets the chance it rare it's ugly head
And no matter where I am in my life
Immediately I am back at ground Zero.
I have tried several therapist and meditation
As my mother would say only time will heal all sorrows.
What has it done with your life?
Haunted by the memories of 911 forever and a day
Lord teach us how to truly pray.

LOSS COLUMBINE

What joy you brought into our lives.
Your first cry, your first smile, what
Beautiful memories.
Your first step, your first fall, your
Favorite toy, your Barbie doll.
The long summer evenings walks in the
Park.
Daycare; you never attended, you never
Had a baby-sitter or a nanny. We took
You everywhere.
I now recall vividly your first day at
Kindergarten school. Although I am still
Confused who started to cry first you or I.
We managed day by day until we both realized
Everything would be all right. School became an
Intricate part of our lives. Then it struck us like
A bolt of lightning, college is on the horizon.
Bang! Bang! Bang! You never heard the
Shots you were fatally wounded.
We are still hoping this is a nightmare and we'll

Wake up soon. Shock, numbness and disbelief.
When you died we all died. Who would commit
Such devious crime? The kid next door. We replace
Prayer with guns.
We tried our best to protect you, your whole life
Fifteen years.
As we watch you asleep in the arms of Jesus today
We have to conclude this matter the Lord giveth and
The Lord taketh, blessed be His name.

MOONLIGHT ON THE BAY

Have you ever noticed the silver silent moon as she creeps quietly through the night, in a city,
No, there is too much artificial lighting.
I have enjoyed many moonlit nights as it so gently
Soothed my black skin on those cool Jamaican nights. Those
Nights when there is not a cloud in sight and our game
Was count your lucky stars and who spotted the great bear
Or big dipper won all the lucky stars.
The nights when the main road for a half mile or so
Became the track field. Competition was high and the prize
Given was first place only.
I never knew I could long for those nights.
To all my fellow Jamaicans especially my country children
Enjoy all of nature's gifts especially those moonlit nights.

MY FIRST TRAUMA EXPERIENCE
(AWARD WINNING ESSAY – CONNECTICUT
HOSPITAL ASSOCIATION – AUGUST 2003

Beep, beep, beep,
The elevator door swung wide open
Orders shouting out everywhere
The intercom was hot
Emergency we need the trauma room. Room eight we yelled
What is it ruptured Abdominal Aortic Aneurysm and loosing pressure
My adrenaline started to flow like the Niagara rapids
I darted down to room eight and within seconds the room was engulfed with medical staff
Surgeons, nurses, technicians, anesthesiologists and residents.
Perspiration running down my face like dewdrops on rose petals at the break of dawn.
Room eight became an instant inferno.
Within nano seconds the patient was prepped from stem to stern
Drapes, towel clips, back table, Mayo stand race across the floor to the
operating table like squirrels scampering for their last nuts.
Suctions off, bovie off. Is the patient grounded?
Scalpel, snap, bovie lets go we have a life to save.
Do we have blood and platelets in the room?
Yes, replied my circulator Sharon; who is frantically completing the ties in back of surgeon gowns.
Organizing the chaos in the room and attending to each need with such grace under fire.
You would be amazed to observe my circulator Sharon prioritizes in such chaos.
Anesthesia how are the vitals, we are about to make that grand entrance.
Are the suctions ready to go, cell saver?
This belly is full of blood. Pshshsh there was dead silence as three liters of blood came oozing out.
Clamp, clamp I handed two aorta clamps large and medium. Good job.

Someone please adjust the lights, I have to stop this bleeding as soon as possible.
Everyone working in synchrony the team was like an orchestra
well rehearsed for a major performance.
Angled Debakey, stitch 3.0 prolene suture, rubber shod, stitch and the process was repeated.
I think we are on to something here.
Slowly the tension in room calmed down like the wind after a severe storm.
You can lower the temperature in the room at least 10 degrees my scrubs are drenched.
I whispered underneath my breath thank you God
As the team worked relentlessly a warm sense of satisfaction
that all of our efforts and quick thinking paid off.
Once again our purpose was validated we saved another life that's why I will never
walk away from my position in the Operating Room as a surgical Technologist.
Caring is a fundamental part of our professional existence.

MY LIST

There are a few things I would like from you Lord in my life.
Where there is despair give me hope.
Where there is pain give me relief.
Where there is sickness give me healing.
Where there is wrath give me peace.
Where there is confusion give me understanding.
Where there is a problem give me a solution.
Where there is sorrow give me joy.
And I shall be like a tree planted by the rivers of water.

OBSERVE

Today I took a stroll down a lonely busy street.
I never noticed the flowers bloom or scented honey
From the bees.
I never noticed the great blue skies and the fluffy
White clouds as they glided by and shadowed the sun
For a moment
I heard birds singing, dogs barking from the animal
Shelter close by, a faint sound of a cats meow.
A beggar asking for one more quarter.
The taxicab driver yelling at an elderly couple as
They shuffled across the busy street.
The truck honking their horns impatiently in a traffic
Jam.
I came to my senses when I noticed four homeless
Men sharing a cup of coffee and a sandwich.
Yes, there is still love in the world.

PARADISE ISLAND JAMAICA

The land of Bamboo trees, mango trees, Coconut trees and guango trees,
The smell of burning cane fields and cane cutters chopping away with the sharpest machetes
you will ever see. There is no taste quite as burnt sugar cane primary school children ahhh.
And trees swaying in the sweet blowing trade winds, the smell of blossoms
in the air, the buzzing of the honey bees and birds singing happily.

Children running bare feet in the mud and rain, playing innocently
Farmer George in his banana stained clothes soaked with Portland
rain, sheltering himself with a large dashine leaf
Winding unpaved country roads without end. Roosters crowing at the
break of dawn, clanging of water pans at the stand pies.
The mist of the morning in race with the sun rising, what unadorned primordial beauty as nature
exchanges night into daylight? That's the Jamaica I remember. The fresh dewdrops soaking
my feet as my mother calls out, out the lamps, light the coal stove. Just give me a moment
to reminisce on those days when children had no care in the world except to be happy.
When the Portland rains fell like monsoons and marched against the zinc top roofs like an army
marching on to war. When drum pans would overflow with water caught from the roof gutters.
When the sun would pop up from nowhere and sine like a diamond in the sky and the banana
trees would glisten at her rays as if they were smiling at her magnificent radiance. That's the
paradise on earth Jamaica. The land of my birth. The land filled with richness of bauxite, minerals,
Rivers like the Rio Grande, Martha Brae for rafting. Swift River, Black River for her uniqueness
and the winding Rio Cobra that runs under the most famous yet dangerous Flat Bridge. The
roadside vendors selling the sweetest East Indian mangoes you will ever eat, navel oranges and
naseberries. The picturesque prime rock, one of a kind in the world mystery. So when you think
of Reggae music, Ackee and Salt fish, Roast breadfruit and Escovitched fish, chocolate tea,
White Rum, Blue Mountain coffee, Seven Miles of white sand beach, the Island for the best
sprinters in the world, and winner of Miss World. The most traveled island people in the world.
This is the land of my birth Jamaica, I will never forget. The Black, Green and Gold.

PATIENCE

As I listened to the waves as they caress the shore in
The stillness of the evening, I wondered deeply how
Patient the waves must have been in the deep
Oceans to make it to the shores.

Yet not knowing what peace and tranquility it gives
To others.
Just listen to the hush sounds it makes when it kisses
The sandy shores.
There is a lot of patience in nature, the rain, the
Snow, the wind, and the sunshine.
How patient is the sun that gives us all the energy
We need to live.
The dawning of new daybreaks.
As I took note of nature's patience, I realized I lost
My patience today.
Just as the sunrises in the east tomorrow is another
day I will try again.

THAT DAY OF DARKNESS

Boom! What an explosion
My world came tumbling down
It seems like a volcanic eruption
Jesus! What in the world is going on?
Engulfed with fear
I froze for out of here
Something terrible is happening
I don't know what it is.
I raced towards the elevators
But the doors did not open
I ran towards the staircases
And literally flew down the steps.
When I came to a halt I was on the tenth floor

Out of breath, but with death staring me straight in my face
I reached down into myself
And ran with all my might
When my feet hit the pavement outside
I felt like a kangaroo being chased by a lion.
Then this haunting silence followed by the most deafening sound I ever heard.
Like forty freight trains racing out of control down the Blue Mountains
All heads in one direction.
What horror it must have been
When the towers came crashing in.
What thoughts refracted through my mind?
As I felt this tremendous wind
The mighty force of terrorism made an indelible mark into
America's democracyism.
It rented our hearts, souls and lives into shredded pieces
Leaving hollow places.
People minds without peace is devastating
We got more than enough to think about
Choking and covered with debris from head to toe.
One shoe on, scared beyond death, no pocketbook
Stockings torn off, blouse wide open all buttons missing
Amazing I came to my senses, I thought for a minute
What am I doing way out here?
Dear GOD help us all
People told me I ran like a mad woman, true because that fateful day 911
I lost my mind, friends, workers and strangers forever.

THE BEAUTY OF DARKNESS

I have never seen the sunrise of the sunset,
But I feel the warmth of its ultra violet rays as it bathes my black skin on a hot summer day.
The lush bright orange sunset, I heard so often described by others.
I can only imagine the serenity of the sunset.

I have heard rain beat like bullets on the roof, children
Playing in the puddles.
I have felt the soft snowflakes against my face, my feet
Buried in the slush it makes as it falls to the ground.
I have heard of barren trees and beautiful leaves in the
Fall, especially in New England. How caressing the leaves feel
beneath my feet as I walk through the park. Imagining.

No one have ever seen the wind not even me, but its power Is phenomenal it
whistles, howls and screams and changes Velocity without notice.
I would love to tell you how much I have seen but it's all in my imagination I am blind.

THE BOMBERS MIND

I packed my knapsack for the last time
Only I knew that of course
I took my special lunch box and
Replaced my favorite sandwich, fruit and drink
With a lunch that could serve a multitude

Ticking away and racing against time
Like a cheetah in the heat of a chase
I boarded the city bus and passed by
My school for the very last time
I saw my friends and some other kids
I really didn't care for playing in the yard
My life of fourteen years not much
Strolled across my mind like a video in reverse
Or car tires revolving at high speed in the movies
My next and final stop was the market place
I walked off the bus as if I was in slow motion
Numb with fear, anxiety and excitement
All wrapped up in one parcel
Or like the mind of a mad man
On a stormy day blown dried leaves
I glanced at all the faces that passed by
And stared at those in the distance
I knew some were innocent and I even stared
At the faces of the unborn yes, babies in the secret
Places of their mother's womb
In a matter of seconds their lives would change forever
Some would join me in paradise or be dammed in hell
Or live in fear, despair and confusion forever
What do you want from me?
I had nothing to live for
I took my last breath and closed my eyes
And vision paradise.

THE LAND OF PLENTY

In the land of plenty
Man goes hungry daily
In the land of plenty
Man walks naked
In The land of plenty
Man is homeless
In the land of plenty
Man is lonely
In the land of plenty
Man is rejected
In the land of plenty
Man is bleeding
In the land of plenty
Man is brokenhearted
In the land of plenty
Man is hopeless
In the land of plenty
Man is neglected
In the land of plenty
Man is lost
In the land of plenty
Man dies of wants and basic needs
In the land of plenty
Who cares in the land of plenty?
Men die of greed,
In the land of plenty.

THE MEMORIES OF HURRICANE KATRINA

My life spiraled like a twin engine jet out of control
To inevitable destruction.
Then suddenly there was a deadly silence
A terrible roar and water came rushing down like
A mighty wind filled river.
We were trapped helplessly in its rage
The city was like a ghost town and it was twilight.
We scrambled to the attic for rescue, as the waters
Rose in her angry rage, like a volcano in her peak season.
This must be like the days of Noah
Absolutely terrifying,
Cars, houses, bodies, animals, coffins and all types of debris
Just drifted by in the dull lunar glow of a horrifying night.
The city was consumed with Mother Nature's force of water
Yet there was none to drink
Minutes become hours, as the fear of death gripped our souls
Like hungry lions on the prairie
Don't stand there on your dry land and criticize and question
Why we did not leave?
We are living paupers; we barely had food for the next meal
A car to drive that never happened in our family, a bank account
Atm card we never had. You think we all have experienced the
"American dream"
We sold garbage like cans and beer bottles
And lived in a third floor walk up apartment on the other side of the

Railroad tracks, you know what I mean. New Orleans was home to me
That's all I ever knew. At nights I'd go play a few tricks with cards
To make a couple dollars.
You think life in America is easy for all people
You have never been poor I suppose.
It seems like daybreak will be here soon, but the silence outside
Is deafening, Its like we are marooned on a deserted island.
I can hear everyone breathing what melody the breath of life carries
I thought to myself I must use my imagination for some pleasant thoughts
And hope for rescue soon.
We gnawed our way to the top of the roof and met the awesome sunrise.
Yes it is anew day Katrina moved on what havoc and memories she took and left behind.

THE RECOVERING ADDICT

The road seems so long
The way so dark
The journey so endless
Why bother to start.

I stumbled for the light
I fell off the path
Everything so hopeless
I feel all apart.

I looked to the hills
From whence cometh my help
The hills looked like volcanoes
Awaiting an eruption.

I grappled, I yelled, I gave up
I died, yes several times within
I heard a small voice whispering
You can make it, you must win.
Cocaine, Crack, Alcohol, Sex, drugs
And addictions are strong
But to the blood of Jesus
We all belong.

Then I awoke with an agonize cry
My clothes soaked with sweat
My hair standing high
My heart beating wild.

And I prayed as I have never prayed before
To be freed from crack cocaine
And the devils power
I must confess I failed the test.

I am an addict bound for hell
Trapped within myself
I reached out for help
With no future in sight.

I rushed to the shelter
Fell down on my face
And cried out help me
Oh God so full of grace.

With tears of joy and hope streaming down my face
I stand before you
Dauntless cleans and free
My addictions in my haunting pass.

At times I wonder how long it will last
Others live one day at a time
I am living one moment at a time
Oh thank you Jesus for your love sublime.

THE SOUNDS OF HISTORY

The journey to Auswicz was awful.
We were thrown in the back of soldier Lorries and herded
like cattle to train stops at the break of dawn.
Children frantically bawling their eyes out, parents confused and separated.
Allowed a few personal belongings like the clothes on our backs.
No pets welcomed who cares?
Hitler, Stalin, Mussolini, who? These men from hell. I thought they were the devil themselves.
Chaos, confusion, desolation. What in the world is going on?

My God, all Jews need to be in concentration camps.
Barbed wire fences, cold cement beds, no sanitation.
We were brought in by the thousands. Old, young, lame, men, women and of course children me.
Cold, wet and starving we dug our own mass graves, oh yes we did.
Like salmon swimming up an Alaskan river we fought desperately to survive.
A handful of us from my camp did.
The gas chambers were real. The torture chambers were unimaginable.
Children dying from loneliness and starvation so painful.

Survival was far from my reach because death had become a very dear and close friend of mine.
The stinking of rotten human flesh that permeated the
atmosphere for miles and months incredible.
How can I forget the thick black smoke that hovered for years after in my memory?
The giant ovens that were used to burn my grandfather, my parents
and so many more Jews that I will never meet.
Some of us died slaving for you, others were killed for your
amusement and you want me to forget the holocaust.

Like black people never want slavery to be forgotten and
American Indians their heritage and lands.
The holocaust is indelible in my mind. It's impossible to erase; I have tried on several occasions.
The nightmares, memories and yes the screaming still haunts me to this day.
I often burst out in cold sweat without notice. My heart takes off
like a bat out of hell and I lose control and weep.

Because sixty years later it feels like moments ago.
I was only ten years old when I had this terrible experience that changed my life forever.
How I survive this, you have to have been there. I hope my re-collection will help you.
I was only a number etched in Hitler's history books.
Asleep one night there was uproar as bodies were thrown unto the back of trucks.
When I realized what was happening they were next to me so I played dead.

You see death had come so many times before so I knew what to do.
The night was dark and very cold. The only hope I had were
a few stars twinkling from way up high.
I could hear orders being yelled out as we traveled over bumpy dirt roads. A few
bodies fell off on the mountainside before we reached our destination.
Suddenly we came to an abrupt stop.

This is it I'm doomed.
Imagine being the only living among all dead. As bodies were thrown from
the trucks thump, thump miraculously I landed close to the top of the
pile. They never felt the little warmth that was left in my body.
By this time the odor was getting the better of me and I wanted
to cough so hard, what pressure I felt within.
I waited for the trucks to pull away and there was no sound but my
heart as it beat vigorously against my bony chest cage.

I felt a divine presence as the bodies on top of me were so
feathers like as I rolled them off me one by one.
I was overwhelmed with fear of being alive.
I began to wander off in the opposite direction alone. Tired and hungry I stopped to take a nap
in no mans land and drifted far away like a lost piece of log after the storm on the ocean.

It seemed like eternity. Hours later I was awaken by marching footsteps.
Trembling like leaves on a blustering fall day, I slowly opened my eyes. There stood
two young soldiers about 19 years old as if they were keeping guard over me.
\They spoke few words softy, run for your life straight ahead and handed me a piece of stale bread.
That was the best piece of bread I had in months.
When I reached the border I used the hand signal and entered a free zone.

Orphaned, confused, lonely and hungry were not the words to describe
the sounds that were coming from my belly and soul.
Where will I find refuge, I can hardly trust anyone.
For the first time in months I heard the laughter of children. Children
Simple things I had forgotten how to laugh.
The children told me they were orphans and that an elderly lady had been caring for
them and they are sure she would not be worried if I came home with them.

So I followed them home timidly.
To be welcomed and drenched into a hot tub felt like heaven.
We sat down for a meal and tears of joy and sorrow streamed
down my face like cascading waterfalls.
Jacob! Are you going to eat 'twas then that I came to my senses,
this is really happening to me. Damn you Hitler.
I survived the holocaust.

TRUE IDENTITY

So I am equally educated as you are with the exact qualifications.
Living in the same upscale neighborhood as yourself
But I am still three fifths of a man
Often referred to as the Negroes, the black family,
The Africans or colored people.
Somewhat ignorant of our God given rights
Probably I should still be physically chained
And bound in slavery.
Or should I be standing half naked on auction blocks,
Hoping for at least the scrapings from your tables
After the dogs have eaten.

It is impossible to get away from these thoughts
That seems so ancient.
Yet so fresh in my mind
I am constantly reminded when
I dare to forget, I am inferior
Yes I am black
My birth mother is white Italian

My black daddy left home when I was born
He could not take the pressures of life and society
Having a white woman in his life
You see society dictates your quantity of misery.

Although I could pass for white
Society reminds me daily, of who my father is,
Black, African American, or when they want me mad a Nigger.

WHO AM I?

Cotton fields, Tobacco fields, Cane fields.
Underneath cloudless skies in the boiling sun.
No food, No rest, No pay.
Africans.

Beaten, Scorned, Spat upon, and Lynched, Hung.
Slaves.

Housekeepers, Nannies, Chauffeurs, Butlers, Gardeners.
Colored.

Street Sweepers, Garbage Collectors, Sanitation Workers,
Dock workers.
Negroes.

Ghettos, Drug Dealers, Jailhouses, Prisons, Guns and
Triggers.
Niggers.

High School Graduates Valedictorians, Colleges Graduates,
Comrades, University Graduates.
Black.

Inventors, Entrepreneurs, Lawyers, Doctors, Policemen,
Athletes, Teachers, Preachers, Computer Technicians,
Politicians.
Yes African Americans.

WHY DON'T YOU TELL ME?

Why don't you tell me?
I was not born a slave but a free man.
Why don't you tell me?
No matter where I come from
I am still black. An African
Why don't you tell me?
I was sold into slavery by my own flesh and blood
Like Joseph brothers did to him way back when.
Why don't you tell me?
We fought many wars on the front line and died
For a country that denied us the right to vote and equal rights
Why don't you tell me?
Like in any other nations, we were mathematicians, scientists,
Lawyers, doctors, teachers and even politicians.
Why don't you tell me we contributed a lot to this?
Motherland of the free and brave America.
Why don't you tell me?

With our own blood sweat and tears we build this great country
Why don't you tell me?
We were exceptional inventors to this modern world.
Why don't you tell me?
About great men like Garrett Morgan who invented the breathing device,
Dr. Carter Goodwin Woodson who made February Black History Month,
Mary McCleod Bethune first black woman to advice four US Presidents
Benjamin Banneker the first black person to receive a presidential appointment .Thurgood
Marshall the first black judge to serve on the supreme court of America.
Why don't you tell me?
About The Rev.Dr. Martin Luther King Jr. who made the ultimate sacrifice so we can vote today.
Why don't you tell me? About men like Marcus Mosiah Garvey born in St.
Ann's Bay Jamaica, who is responsible for the workers unions of today. The
International World of Arts will never forget the artist Robert Nesta Marley "Bob
Marley"Jamaican born who brought the Reggae rhythm to the world..
Yes Arthur Napoleon Robinson born in Trinidad who wrote laws for the
United Nations of the World and is the president Of Trinidad.
How could I forget one of the world's greatest cricketers Gary Sobers born in Guyana and
played for years with the West Indies cricket team, setting records until his retirement?
Why don't you tell me?
About Kwame Nkrumah from Ghana .Sekou Toure from Guinea, Jomo
Kenyatta of Kenya, Julius Kamborage Nyrere of Tanzania. All these great men
who were the founding fathers of the organization of African Unity.
Why don't you tell me?
I came from royalty.
Why don't you tell me?
About Kunta Kente, Ayuba, Kwasi, Naiobe and the many children
of Mother Africa who languished and died in my place.
Why don't you tell me?

About Nelson Mandella from South Africa who spent thirty long, lonely, and trying years imprisoned. Yes and through it all he kept the faith of Job knowing that one day the same JESUS that saved yesterday is the same today and forever.
So we as a people celebrating our African Caribbean heritage today will learn to hold our peace and stand still and see the salvation of the Lord today.
The battle is not ours it's the Lords.

The beautiful heart of Janice Hart

Published: Thursday January 10, 2013 | 12:06 pm

Some of the recipients of Janice Hart's Xmas donations to the Hillside Homeless Shelter in New Haven, CT.

http://jamaica-gleaner.com/extra/article.php?id=1942

Deon Brown
NYC:

In Jamaica's diaspora circles, she's known as 'Mattie Lou', the cultural godchild of folk mistress Miss Lou, and as such a serious advocate of the gospel of Jamaican arts and heritage.

In New Haven County in Connecticut where she has made her home for the last 24 years, she's Janice Hart, the woman with indeed the kind heart. She's not Connecticut wealthy or even a Jamaican with a little change.

What she has is a charitable spirit that has seen her giving of her time and modest means to marginalized communities and struggling families in her resident districts of Hamden and New Haven.

DISPLACED FAMILIES

For the last five years, Hart has adopted a homeless shelter, the Hillside Family Shelter, where she has assisted displaced families with clothing, food, toiletries, household effects and other personal items.

Throughout the year she collects a wide range of goods from friends and associates who will periodically clean out their closets, and she then donates these to various shelters. Many homeless people come to the shelters with next to nothing, and are grateful for the donations.

"When people have things in very good condition, wash and laundered, I take them. I collect blankets, sheets, washcloth, towels, sweaters, coats, cutlery, drinking glasses - a lot of stuff. Last summer I took sixty garbage bags of supplies to Hillside as well as canned goods," Ms Hart revealed.

She's a one-woman committee on a mission of service to the underserved. She was first invited by a friend several years ago to visit the Hillside Homeless Shelter in New Haven and was struck by the stark conditions of the children's existence.

She decided to personally assist a few of them deemed in greatest need with clothing and other necessities after speaking with the center's director. But when one of the surgeons at her job at Yale New Haven Hospital offered financial assistance, she was able to extend her efforts by purchasing supplies for all forty children at the shelter instead of the previously selected seven. She also gave them surprise gifts that first year.

"I got their names, sizes, ages and I got each of them self-wrapped gifts," Hart said. Shelters are transition stations where different homeless families cycle through every few months. As such, Hart has really helped more families than she can count.

Friends and co-workers have joined her cause, and in December she was able to bring some 600 self-wrapped gifts to the children at Hillside. Some of her friends even donated gift cards for the older children. "One ripple can really make an ocean," Hart who hails from Portland, Jamaica stated.

A lot of people have kind hearts, sometime all you have to do is ask...When I think of how fortunate I am, to how less fortunate other people are, I think that's what really drives me to reach out and help others, especially children." It's her go-getter, take-charge personality that gets the job done.

She's the President of the Mutual Respect Committee at her workplace and has used her office to lead a can collection drive and was therefore able to donate 1900 pounds of canned and non-perishable goods to a number of New Haven shelters recently. "I tell each person just bring me one item on the list.

They don't have to bring a grocery bag. We have over 10,000 employees in our hospital system. If I get one can from each person then I've collected a lot of cans," she calculated. In Jamaican parlance, 'one, one cocoa, full basket'.

A woman always on the go, Hart also volunteers at a half-way house in New Haven called The Connection, where men and women who were incarcerated are temporarily placed as part of their transition back to regular society.

She has taught a 12-step type program called 'Critical Decision-Making' where inmates take an introspective examination of their lives and make plans for improvements.

But what has also really distinguished her service there is her cooking where Hart is known to throw down a Jamaican style Thanksgiving meal or Christmas dinner each year.

2012 was no exception. With the financial assistance of two friends, Dr. Roberta Hines, an anesthesiologist at Yale New Haven Hospital and Denise Peacock, Ms Hart provided a multi-dish Christmas feast for the sixty men at The Connection shelter that could have fed Jesus and his flock of five thousand.

She also volunteers at another half-way place called Columbus House and has donated toiletries to them. In addition, she has started another collection drive for soldiers in Afghanistan and has already mailed two boxes of travel size items of toothpaste, deodorant, lotion, breath mints, hand sanitizers and other toiletries.

It is no wonder her family calls her 'Mother Teresa'. Next to her cultural performances, Miss Hart is known for her love of the kitchen. Her culinary skills are legendary, and no one leaves her home without an offer of food and a taste of her delightful concoctions.

Amazingly, she does all the cooking even for the huge shelter meals in her small home kitchen. "If I get somebody to donate a six-burner Viking stove I would really cook up a storm," she says with a laugh.

At the prodding of friends, she has compiled some of her recipes into a book which will be published later this year. So when you see the always well-dressed Janice 'Mattie Lou' Hart wielding through Connecticut communities, in either her clergy apparel (she's an ordained minister) or her beautifully inspired African or Jamaican cultural wear, know that she is a sister on a mission of service, demonstrating what it means to love thy neighbor as thyself and truly be thy brother's keeper. It's the Christ-like message that shines through all year in this wonderful Portland woman's heart.

http://jamaica-gleaner.com/extra/article.php?id=1942

SONS OF THE SOIL

TRIBUTE TO ONE OF THE PIONEERING JAMAICANS WHO IMMIGRATED TO THE USA IN THE 1943, as a farmer worker. Brownie told me the stories how they were referred to in those days, as "British Subjects." How much they struggled to settle in a strange land. They were encouraged by each other and formed a social club in Hartford that is today known as the West Indian Social club of Hartford Inc. The oldest of its kind in the North East

CLEVELAND SAMUEL REID
September 30, 1917- March 15, 2015
AKA "BROWNIE"

NARCISO F. AIREY

One of our living pioneers at 93 years of age, still dances with feet as lite as feather. He migrated to the USA in early 1950's as a farm worker in Hartford, working on Tobacco fields. He still reminds us of the history of their journey, from British Subjects to American Citizens. Mr. Airey or affectionately called Daddy, loves his culture and is present at every possible event, from Canada to Baltimore, Maryland. His daughter Veronica says he is always ready to go, dressed in his tuxedo.

NATIONAL
HEROES

A BRIEF INTRODUCTION OF JAMAICA'S SEVEN NATIONAL HEROES

Information in this document courtesy of Jamaica Information Service.

Brief history of Jamaica. Jamaica's first inhabitants were the Tainos, an Arawak-speaking people, believed to be originally from South America. The Tainos called the island "Xaymaca" meaning "land of wood and water". These peaceful, seafaring people greeted Christopher Columbus when he first visited the island on May 5, 1494. This occurred on his second voyage to the West Indies. The rest is history, Columbus discovered Paradise on earth one hundred and forty four square miles. Three county's Cornwall, Middlesex and Surrey. Fourteen parishes, Kingston, St. Andrew, St. Catherine, St. Thomas. Portland. St. Mary, St. Ann, Manchester, Clarendon, Trewlany, St. James, Hanover, St. Elizabeth, Westmoreland

A national Hero is a person who makes a significant contribution to the development of a society and is admired for any of a number of qualities including courage, outstanding achievements and most times paying the ultimate sacrifice, death.
Jamaica's seven National Heroes have surpassed such qualifications. They challenged colonization in the early centuries and changed the landscape of Jamaica forever. In truth they were warriors in their own rights. They fought for liberty, freedom and justice for all. They were every concerned with humanity and how Jamaicans were treated by the British and all others that had influenced our society in those days. They gave the people of Jamaica social and political freedom. Today our National Heroes Park located in Kingston, Jamaica is a daily reminder to the place in our History for our Heroes.

QUEEN NANNY OF THE MAROONS

Your strength and mystery entwined our history like prophets of old, no one really knows your origin or so the story is told, one thing for certain you are a product of the Motherland of Africa hailing from the Ivory coast of Ghana around the time of 1680, You were bound for a country who laid quietly beneath the shades of the Caribbean sun and the mystical blue seas, the land of wood and water and the days of sun shining on the lush plantations magnificently, Or in the hills of Portland where mother nature rains like English bullets on the thatched roofs, Nanny you came in search of your Ashanti people to set them free from the hands of oppressive slave masters, just has Moses was sent by God to release his people from the slave masters of Egypt and yet they murmured and some doubted his authenticity and power, But when God bestows his blessings and power on you no one can remove it, Imagine an African woman of your statue tall thin and wirery, full of vigor and mystery an army all by yourself, It is said that you had brothers and you were even married but had no children, I am not surprised a woman so occupied with the thoughts of plotting to free her people by defeating the most intelligent and fortified British army of your time was impossible to everyone except you, I believe you knew that scripture that reads where two or three are gathered in my name agreeing as in touching you will be in the midst to Bless, and all things are possible to all those who believe, I don't think you needed a consultant to assist you in devising your tactics and plot, you were simply guided by divine power.

During the late 17th and early 18th centuries Nanny an escaped slave and her four brothers is said to have been slaves from Western Africa, Ghana that were brought to Jamaica. Nanny, known as Granny Nanny, Grandy Nanny and Queen Nanny was a Maroon leader and Obeah woman in Jamaica Nanny of the Maroons stands out in history as the only female among Jamaica's national heroes. Her birthdate is not known. Although small in stature, Nanny possessed that fierce fighting spirit generally associated with the courage of men. In fact, Nanny is described as a fearless Ashanti warrior who used militarist techniques to foul and beguile the English. Captain William Cuffee, known as Captain Sambo, is been credited as killing Nanny in 1733 during one of the many wars she fought. This particular war lasted from 1720 until truce was declared in 1739. Cudjoe, one of Nanny' brothers and a leader during the Maroon War, was the driving force behind the Treaty. Nanny Town was eventually captured by the British and destroyed in 1734. Yet, the spirit of Nanny of the Maroons remains today as a symbol of that indomitable desire that will never yield to captivity. Her image is represented on Jamaica's Five Hundred Dollar Note

PAUL BOGLE

Paul Bogle birthdate is uncertain, he was born between 1815-1820 and died October 24, 1865 .It is said he was born in Stony Guts St. Thomas.

Paul Bogle, a Baptist Deacon was generally regarded as a peaceful man who shunned violence. He believed in the teachings of the Bible, endorsing the principles of charity and endurance. Yet he was also a leader and organizer who knew well the terrains of the land and had spent time in educating and training his followers. During the oppressive years in the early 1850's-1860's Bogle was extremely active in revolting against the system of government. On October 11, 1865 Paul Bogle marched with about three hundred men in Morant Bay, where the Town Council was in session. There they raided the Police Station for arms and the Court House was set on fire. They killed the Custos, Baron Von Ketelhodt and fifteen vestrymen. Bogle lost his life along with most of his men, however he accomplished changes forever.

His image is represented on the original Jamaican two dollars paper note. Today these notes are no longer in use. I recall as a child attending Titchfield High School in Port Antonio, Portland Jamaica, that would have paid my bus fare for a whole week and I would have change left over to buy food. And that was not so long ago.

GEORGE WILLIAM GORDON

George William Gordon (1820-1865) was born near Mavis Bank in the Parish of Saint Thomas in 1820 to Joseph Gordon, a Scottish Plantation Owner and a slave woman. He was the second of eight children. At the age of ten years George went to live with his Godfather, James Daly in Black River saint Elizabeth Jamaica. While living with his Godfather he was mostly self-educated. George began his life as an Anglican parish member but later changed to the Baptist Religion. It is recorded that he was baptized by Rev. J.M. Phillippo, the founder of Jamaica's first "Free Village". He later became a leader of the Native Baptist Movement and began building several churches at his own expense. He ordained Ministers and was a very active Evangelist in those days. In 1843 when he was 23 years old he was elected to the House of Assembly for Saint Thomas. As a member of the House of Parliament, he used his position to highlight the sufferings of the people and to make a plea for changes. George was upset with the conditions of the poorer class of Jamaicans and spoke out loudly on their behalf which was not appreciated and or accepted by the then Lieutenant Governor Edward Eyre. The Morant Bay Rebellion in 1865 and the resultant deaths of Bogle and Gordon precipitated the beginning of a new era in Jamaica's development. The British government became compelled to make changes including outstanding reforms in education, health, local government, banking and infrastructure.

On October 27, 1960, the Jamaican Parliament named the building, where the Parliament meetings are kept, The George William Gordon House, affectionately called "Gordon House" After Independence he was given the nation's highest honor, Order of National Hero.

His image is represented on the original Jamaican Ten dollar paper note. These notes are not in circulation today. Coins are used instead.

SAMUEL "SAM" SHARPE

Samuel Sharpe- AKA - Archer (1801- May 23, 1832), He was the slave leader behind the widespread Jamaican Baptist War slave rebellion of 1832(also known as the Christmas Rebellion Sharpe became a well- known preacher and leader in the Baptist Church, which had long welcomed slaves as members and recognized them as preachers. He was a Deacon at the Burchell Baptist Church in Montego Bay, whose Pastor was Rev. Thomas Burchell, a missionary from England. Sharpe spent most of his time travelling to different parishes in Jamaica, educating the slaves about Christianity, which he believed promised freedom.

'Daddy' Sam Sharpe, as he was affectionately called was to carry on the Resistance against slavery effecting at the young age of 31, the most outstanding Slave Rebellion in Jamaica's history. Sharpe, an educated town slave, was a preacher and spokesman. Intelligent and sharp, he followed the developments of the abolition movement by reading discarded local and foreign papers and was able to advise his followers. Sharpe was tired of slavery, spent months in strategic planning, educating the slaves and traveling from estate to estate in secret meetings at nights, igniting the slaves with inspiring messages of hope of freedom. The 1831 Christmas Rebellion started in St. James and spread throughout the entire island. The Rebellion started on December 28 and lasted 8 days. Sam Sharpe was eventually captured and hung at the Parade in Montego Bay (now renamed Sam Sharpe Square) Just before Sharpe was executed for his role in the rebellion, he said in his last words. "I would rather die among yonder gallows, than live in slavery". On August 28, 1833 slavery was abolished and the System of Apprenticeship instituted, allowing for the total freedom of slaves in the next 4-6 years.

On August 1, 1938 the Apprenticeship System ended granting full freedom to the slaves.

His image is represented on the Jamaican Fifty dollar paper note. Today coins are used instead of the paper notes.

SIR ALEXANDER BUSTAMANTE

Alexander Bustamante (1884-1977) was born as Alexander Clarke to Mary (nee Wilson) and her husband Robert Constantine Clarke, an Irish Catholic planter, in Hanover Jamaica, He took the surname Bustamante to honor a Spanish sea Captain who befriended him in his youth. Bustamante traveled the world and worked in many different places. His occupations included working as a policeman in Cuba and as a dietician in a New York City Hospital. At the age of forty eight he returned to Jamaica in 193.2 Bustamante was an aggressive, outspoken young man who understood the dynamics of labor relations. A charismatic and impressive speaker, he used the media to criticize the prevailing political system and its attendant social problems. He started the Industrial Trade Union in 1938 and was jailed for 17 months following labor riots. He became Jamaica's first Chief Minister, a position he held until 1954, being knighted that same year by the queen.

On August 6, 1962 Jamaica was granted full independence. At the first session of Parliament, Bustamante received the Instruments of Independence from the queen's representative, Princess Margaret. This time in Jamaica's history drastic changes were heralded, not by bloodshed but by peaceful negotiations. Sir Alexander Bustamante was the first Prime Minister of Independent Jamaica. His image is represented on the original One dollar paper note. Today coins are used instead of the paper notes.

NORMAN WASHINGTON MANLEY

Norman Washington Manley (1893-1969) was born in Roxborough, Manchester Jamaica to Thomas Albert Samuel Manley and Margaret Shearer. Norman was a brilliant scholar, soldier and athlete and studied law at Jesus College Oxford as a Rhode Scholar. He served in the Royal Field Artillery during World War 1, and was awarded the Military Medal(M.M.)Norman Manley founded the People's National Party which later was tied to the Trade Union Congress and the N.W. U. Together with Bustamante, their efforts resulted in the New Constitution of 1944 granting full Adult Suffrage. Manley served as the colony's Chief Minister from 1955 to 1959, and as premier from 1959 to 1962He was a proponent of self-government but was persuaded to join nine other British colonies in the Caribbean territories in a Federation of the West Indies, but called for a referendum on the issue in 1961. The 400 year British Rule, invoking slavery, deculturisation, uprising and bloodshed was now at an end.

Due to respiratory illness, Manley retired from politics on his birthday in 1969. He died later that same year, on September 2, 1969. His image is represented on the original Jamaican five dollar paper note. These notes are not in circulation today. Coins are used instead.

MARCUS MOSIAH GARVEY

Marcus Mosiah Garvey (1887-1940) was born on August 17, 1887, in St. Ann's Bay on the north coast of Jamaica. He was the last of eleven children born to Marcus Garvey, Sr. and Sarah Jane Richards. His father was a stone mason and his mother a domestic worker and farmer. His father was a great influence on young Marcus. He once described him as "severe, firm, determined, bold, and strong, refusing to yield even to superior forces if he believed he was right." His father was known to have a large library, where young Garvey learned to read. Garvey stands out in history as one who was greatly committed to the concept of the Emancipation of minds. He became famous worldwide as a leader who was courageous and eloquent in his call for improvement for Blacks. He sought the unification of all Blacks through the establishment of the United Negro Improvement Association and spoke out against economic exploitation and cultural denigration. He spent many years in the United States pursuing his goal of Black Unification.

He left Jamaica in 1910 for Central America, settling first in the coastal town of Limon, Costa Rica, where he published a small newspaper. He also spent time in Honduras and Belize and published another small paper in Panama. After returning to Jamaica briefly in 1912, he left again in 1913 when he moved to England and worked with enigmatic Sudanese-Egyptian nationalist Duse Mohamed Ali, in London. Upon his arrival in America the spring of 1916, Garvey still made a pilgrimage to the world-famous Tuskegee School in Alabama to see firsthand the monument to Washington's memory. This was the era of "New Negro", blacks' discontent punctuated by East St. Louis's bloody race riots in 1917 and intensified by postwar disillusionment, reached record heights by 1919 with the Red Summer of nationwide racial disturbances.

Under Garvey's influence, nearly one thousand UNIA divisions were formed throughout North and Central America, the Caribbean, Africa and Britain as well as a lone division in Australia. By the late 1920's, the movement had begun to unravel under the strain of internal dissension, opposition from black critics, and government harassment. Fiscal irregularities in the shipping line gave the United States government- spurred on by the young Central Intelligence Agency Director J. Edgar Hoover- the basis for an indictment that sent Garvey to prison. The government later commuted Garvey's sentence, only to deport him to Jamaica in November 1927.

The impact of Garveyism in Africa was considerable, although Garvey never set foot on the soil of Africa. Garvey's legacy has also been manifested in the careers of leaders ranging from Kwame Nkrumah of Ghana to Malcolm X. His influence on the Jamaican Rastafarian Religion, Black Islam. His influence on Jamaica Reggae music with artists like Bob Marley, Peter Tosh, Burning Spear and many more.

Some of Marcus Garvey famous quotes" Be not deceived. Wealth is strength, wealth is power, wealth is influence, wealth is justice, is liberty, is real human rights" "there are two classes of men in the world, those who succeed and those who do not succeed." "Hungry men have no respect for law, authority or human life." "If you have no confidence in self you are twice defeated in the race of life. With confidence you have won even before you have started."

Marcus Mosiah Garvey was the first National hero of Jamaica. His image is represented on the original Fifty cent paper note. Today these notes are not in circulation, coins are used instead.

Miss Matty Lou sharing her Ancestory collection at **The Taste of The Caribbean Festival in Hartford, CT**

CARRY MI ACKEE GOH AH LINSTEAD MARKET, NOT A QUATTY WUT SELL
(Photos courtesy of William Clark)

WHEN HARRY MET MISS MATTIE LOU